Cambridge Elements ≡

Elements in Publishing and Book Culture
edited by
Samantha Rayner
University College London
Leah Tether
University of Bristol

PUBLISHING ROMANCE FICTION IN THE PHILIPPINES

Jodi McAlister
Deakin University
Claire Parnell
University of Melbourne
Andrea Anne Trinidad
Ateneo de Manila University

CAMBRIDGE
UNIVERSITY PRESS

Shaftesbury Road, Cambridge CB2 8EA, United Kingdom

One Liberty Plaza, 20th Floor, New York, NY 10006, USA

477 Williamstown Road, Port Melbourne, VIC 3207, Australia

314–321, 3rd Floor, Plot 3, Splendor Forum, Jasola District Centre,
New Delhi – 110025, India

103 Penang Road, #05–06/07, Visioncrest Commercial, Singapore 238467

Cambridge University Press is part of Cambridge University Press & Assessment,
a department of the University of Cambridge.

We share the University's mission to contribute to society through the pursuit of
education, learning and research at the highest international levels of excellence.

www.cambridge.org
Information on this title: www.cambridge.org/9781009096430

DOI: 10.1017/9781009092289

© Jodi McAlister, Claire Parnell and Andrea Anne Trinidad 2023

First published 2023

A catalogue record for this publication is available from the British Library.

ISBN 978-1-009-09643-0 Paperback
ISSN 2514-8524 (online)
ISSN 2514-8516 (print)

Publishing Romance Fiction in the Philippines

Elements in Publishing and Book Culture

DOI: 10.1017/9781009092289

First published online: May 2023

Jodi McAlister
Deakin University

Claire Parnell
University of Melbourne

Andrea Anne Trinidad
Ateneo de Manila University

Author for correspondence: Jodi McAlister, jodi.mcalister@deakin.edu.au

ABSTRACT: The romance publishing landscape in the Philippines is vast and complex, characterised by entangled industrial players, diverse kinds of texts, and siloed audiences. This Element maps this large, multilayered, and highly productive sector of the Filipino publishing industry. It explores the distinct genre histories of romance fiction in this territory and the social, political, and technological contexts that have shaped its development. It also examines the close connections between romance publishing and other media sectors alongside unique reception practices. It takes as a central case study the Filipino romance self-publishing collective #RomanceClass, analysing how they navigate this complex local landscape as well as the broader international marketplace. The majority of scholarship on romance fiction exclusively focuses on the Anglo-American industry. By focusing here on the Philippines, the authors hope to disrupt this phenomenon and to contribute to a more decentred, rhizomatic approach to understanding this genre world.

KEYWORDS: romance fiction, romanceclass, Filipino romance, popular fiction, publishing studies

ISBNs: 9781009096430 (PB), 9781009092289 (OC)

ISSNs: 2514-8524 (online), 2514-8516 (print)

Contents

Introduction   1

1   The Filipino Romance Publishing Industry   12

2   Filipino Romance Texts: From Tagalog
Pocketbooks to #RomanceClass   34

3   Collectivity and Care: The Case of #RomanceClass
Sociality   57

Conclusion: Decentralising Romance Fiction   76

References   80

Introduction

Imagine a family living in Pasig, a district in Metro Manila that hosts a mix of office buildings, upscale housing, large shopping malls, museums, cathedrals, and parks that hold markets on weekends. Three generations of women in this family live together in a large apartment and share a love for romance fiction.

Despite their common interest in the genre, as romance readers and consumers, they are very different. The eldest of the three women reads romance novels written in Taglish (a code-mixing vernacular of Tagalog and English) that she purchases at the local convenience store down the street. Her favourites feature young girls from poverty-stricken areas of the Philippines being swept off their feet by rich heroes from the heart of Manila.

Her daughter, who benefited from a middle-class education in the late twentieth century, prefers more progressive romances. A few years ago, a friend of hers shared a Facebook post about an event at Estancia, their local mall, hosted by a local self-publishing community, where actors read passages from contemporary romance novels. She attended with her friend, bought some of the books being sold on a table at the side of the room, and began reading as soon as she was home. Now, she buys most of her romances published by this group from their website. She reads them avidly – when she's not worrying about the amount of time her daughter spends on her smartphone.

But when she's on her smartphone, her daughter is also reading romance. She's in her second year of high school, so she doesn't have a lot of disposable income to spend on the paperback books her mother and grandmother read, but everyone in her school is *obsessed* with a new romance story on Wattpad. She reads it on her phone as she walks to school, between classes, at lunchtime, and late at night once she's finished her homework. She's considering posting her own story to the platform under a pseudonymous username. For inspiration, she's planning to buy a copy of a book by her all-time favourite Wattpad author at the National Bookstore at Estancia, which was published in paperback form through a partnership between the platform and a traditional Philippine publishing house.

Here, we can see a glimpse of the dynamism of the Filipino romance publishing landscape, which encompasses very different practices of creation, production, distribution, and reception. There are numerous distinct kinds of popular romance fiction in the Philippines, ranging from traditionally published Tagalog pocketbook romances to self-published English-language romances produced by #RomanceClass; traditionally published English-language chick lit to young adult (YA) romance published on digital platforms in a variety of Filipino languages and dialects.

These distinctive publishing modes are frequently entangled. For example, many of the large traditional romance publishers in the Philippines have partnerships with and/or run their own digital platforms for the purposes of discoverability, acquisition, and/or sales. Similarly, some self-published authors in #RomanceClass began their careers publishing chick lit with traditional publishers. In other instances, though, these publishing modes are quite dispersed, sometimes defined in opposition to one another. Romance fiction in the Philippines is also closely connected to the platform and entertainment media industries and encompasses diverse and unique Filipino reception practices. Providing a detailed picture of this complicated sector of publishing and book culture is a primary aim of this Element.

This Element represents the first extended study of romance fiction in the Philippines in the twenty-first century. Previously, Patricia May B. Jurilla examined Tagalog romance fiction in the late twentieth century as part of her book history of bestsellers in the Philippines, examining its emergence from other Filipino popular genres like metrical romances (2008; see also Reyes, 1991). Jurilla's study, which concludes in 2003, serves as a foundation for this Element. We take up where she left off, examining Filipino romance fiction publishing in the 'long twenty-first century', a term that Rachel Noorda and Stevie Marsden have argued is appropriate in order to capture the organisational and technological developments of the late twentieth century that have significantly shaped book publishing and culture in the twenty-first century (2019: 6). As we will explore, romance in the Philippines is closely connected with traditional media institutions and platform companies. As such, our research combines a book history approach with contemporary publishing studies as it intersects with media and platforms studies: a new and, we hope, exciting set of intersecting approaches to popular romance. This is also among the first pieces of sustained scholarship to focus on a romance publishing ecosystem outside of the dominant Anglo-American publishing industry. By examining Filipino romance fiction published in the Philippines for a mostly Filipino market, we hope to contribute to decolonisation efforts in publishing and popular romance studies through decentring the West.

Researching romance fiction in the Philippines is not without its challenges. It encompasses a dispersed ecosystem of production models, media forms, and reception sites and practices. In addition to this dispersion, there is little research on romance publishing, or even book publishing more broadly, in the Philippines. Jurilla notes that the history of the book in the Philippines 'has not yet arrived. It is a territory that is still largely unexplored if not totally unheard of in Philippine scholarship' (2008: 5). This presents significant challenges but also exciting opportunities to scholars who seek to investigate any part of this industry landscape. As Jurilla describes, 'the terrain to cover is immense, the journey quite lonely and rough at this point' (2008: 10). There are significant gaps in the scholarly literature and an 'enormous amount of basic archival and bibliographic work remains to be done on all aspects of print and publishing throughout Philippine history' (Jurilla, 2008: 10). Romance fiction suffers a double invisibility in Philippine book publishing scholarship, often overlooked in favour of more serious and canonical literature. However, despite the minimal attention paid, Filipino romance publishing is a vibrant and thriving sector of book culture – as we intend to explore here.

Researching Romance Fiction

Romance is a significant genre for study. Globally, romance publishing is a billion-dollar industry, and the sheer volume of romance novels published is something often emphasised in scholarly discussions of the genre, frequently as a justification for taking them seriously (Fletcher *et al.*, 2019; McAlister *et al.*, 2020). Their popularity in the Philippines is likewise reflected in their bestselling status. As Jurilla notes, romance novels have been the nation's literary bestsellers (2008).

However, the fact that romance books are popular and sell in high numbers is not the only justification for their study: as Wilkins *et al.* argue, romance, and genre fiction more broadly, 'is more than a commercial phenomenon' (2022: 23). The romance fiction sector has been at the forefront of technological innovation and is highly adaptive to industry changes. The genre has adapted more swiftly to changing technological and market practices than any other genre (Markert, 1985; 2016; Tapper, 2014). It leads the way in the number of self-published titles and was a principal factor in the uptake and popularisation of e-books and e-readers (Driscoll *et al.*, 2018; Fletcher *et al.*, 2018; Parnell, 2018). In Australia, for instance, romance fiction has experienced the highest rate of growth in self-published titles from 2000 to 2016, compared to fantasy and crime fiction (Driscoll *et al.*, 2018; Fletcher *et al.*, 2018). Scholars and industry practitioners attribute the genre's willingness to diversify content, experiment with multiple subgenres and hybrid genres, and cultivate new readerships and online channels for reader communities for its continued growth in the early twenty-first century (Cuthbert, 2021; Parnell, 2021; Wilkins *et al.*, 2022).

A key part of romance fiction's growth has been in 'diverse' romance: that is, romance which features characters from racially and/or otherwise marginalised backgrounds, often written by authors from that background. Alongside this has been the growth of a body of scholarship which focuses on it, usually centring on textual representations in various subgenres: for example, desert or sheikh romances (Bach, 1997; Burge, 2016; Burge & Folie, 2021; Jarmakani, 2020; Taylor, 2007; Teo, 2012), Indian romance (Bohidar, 2021; Kamblé, 2007; Rudisill, 2018; Uparkar, 2014), African American romance (Dandridge, 2010; 2022; Hendricks, 2022; Hendricks & Moody-Freeman, 2022; Huguley, 2022; Jackson, 2022; Moody-Freeman, 2020; 2022; Pritchard, 2022; Tindall, 2022), Muslim romance (Abdullah-Poulos, 2018; Parnell, 2022), Chinese web fiction romance (Feng, 2021), and, of course, Filipino romance fiction (Barrios, 2001; Jurilla, 2008; McAlister *et al.*, 2020; Parnell *et al.*, 2021a; Parnell *et al.*, 2021b; Santiago, 2009). However, with only a few exceptions, these studies still tend to be rooted in the dominant North American publishing industry, centring authors and readers in an English-speaking Western context. Indeed, this is arguably inherent in the idea of 'diversity' itself: the paradigm it seeks to complicate is one of hegemonic, usually American, Whiteness. While it is impossible to escape the influence of the dominant Anglo-American industry, in this Element we hope to make a different kind of contribution by approaching the Filipino romance publishing ecosystem in its own context and on its own terms: specifically, as a distinctive genre world.

The Social, Economic, and Political Context of Filipino Romance Publishing and Reading

The historical and current social, economic, and political conditions of the Philippines greatly impact its publishing culture. The country's history of colonisation and its ongoing impacts on class and language, the dictatorship of President Ferdinand Marcos (1965–86) and implementation of martial law (formally 1972–81), as well as the unequal wealth distribution that is deeply ingrained in Filipino society, all influence how romance continues to be published, distributed, and received.

The Philippines has one of the highest wealth gaps between high and low socio-economic populations in Southeast Asia, and this is further widened by the country being prone to climate change disasters and the related socio-economic losses (Ong, 2015: 3). A five-level classification system (Classes A–E) is often used to describe the various socio-economic income segments of the Philippine population, which are based on 'income, wealth, assets and overall living conditions' (Deinla & Dressel, 2019: 17). Classes A and B are used to refer to those who belong to the upper class; Class C describes those who are part of the middle class, which is further divided between C1 (upper-middle class) and C2 (lower-middle class); and Classes D and E those who are among the lower class (Uy-Tioco, 2019: 159). Various classes are often combined in statistical data depending on their relative size and political power; Classes A and B (and sometimes C), for example, are often counted together due to the small number of upper-class households in the Philippines (7 per cent in 2019, according to the Social Weather Stations survey) (Mangahas, 2022). As with several other countries worldwide, working- and lower-class citizens make up the majority of the population in the Philippines: Class D represented 75 per cent of the population in 2019 and Class E 18 per cent (Mangahas, 2022).

The socio-economic make-up of the Philippines has been an influential factor in the production and reception of romance fiction throughout the twentieth and early twenty-first centuries. Tagalog romance fiction has become a hugely popular genre due to publishers enthusiastically targeting readers from Class D and E income segments. This target market has contributed to romance's commercial success because of the sheer numbers in this market, despite their relatively low purchasing power (Ong, 2015). Conscious of their readers' spending capacity, traditional Tagalog pocket-book romance publishers have been strategic in their inclusion of particular narrative tropes, production design, and pricing in order to make them widely accessible to the majority of the population. According to the 2017 National Book Development Board (NBDB) Readership Survey, 75.7 per cent of Filipinos were willing to spend PHP 199 (US$3.58) for non-school-related e-books, and 72.54 per cent were willing to spend the same for books published by Filipino publishers. Bookware Publishing Corporation, a leading publisher in Tagalog pocketbook romances that launched in 1992, is emphatic in its intention to maintain My Special Valentine Romances – its flagship series/imprint of Tagalog romances – at 'price points at levels that are affordable to a greater segment of its target market – the C, D and E income groups' (Bookware Publishing Corporation, 2022). At the time of writing, Bookware's catalogue shows a range of romance novels priced between PHP 29.00 (US$0.51) and PHP 199.75 (US$3.49). They also offer more affordable 8-peso (US$0.14) e-books on their online store. Although the country has a 'patchy' economic record 'with regular boom and bust cycles' (Deinla & Dressel, 2019: 1), Tagalog pocketbook romances continue to make affordability and accessibility for their audience a top priority, providing enough remuneration for their authors and profitable ventures that make business expansions possible for their publishers.

In addition to price, there is also a complex interplay of language, class, and taste between the romance genre and its Filipino audience. Writing in English has been an established mode of literary production in the Philippines, rooted in America's colonisation of the country in the first half of the twentieth century. The first book to be printed entirely in English was published just twenty years after colonisation (Abinales, 1981: 19–20). English was the primary language of instruction in formal educational settings between 1901 and 1974, which resulted in English-language titles – historically produced for and marketed to middle- and upper-class audiences who could afford this kind of education – dominating the publishing industry until the late twentieth century (Gonzales, 2004; Tupas, 2019). English has maintained its 'class-ifying' and 'stratifying' role in Filipino society (Tupas, 2019: 538), with the language often seen as a 'wedge' that separated 'educated Filipinos from the masses of their countrymen' (Constantino, 1970: 24). At present, this divide operates not just in public spaces – where wet markets, neighbourhood stores, and middle-class establishments such as Robinson's and SM malls use Filipino, whereas five-star establishments, hotels, and restaurants use English (Gonzales, 2004) – but also in reading spheres, between the audiences of Tagalog pocketbook romance and Filipino romance in English. The ability to speak, read, and write in English has historically reflected a privileged social position in Filipino society and this legacy remains to various degrees in different spheres of cultural production. While some Tagalog romance authors can achieve tremendous popularity – a kind of 'rock star' status among readers – writers who publish in English still receive a greater level of respect (Radyo Katipunan 87.9, 2021).

The Genre World of Filipino Romance

The genre worlds model, as theorised by Kim Wilkins, Beth Driscoll, and Lisa Fletcher, examines popular genres through a tripartite focus on interlinked parts: industrial processes, social formations, and textual conventions (2022). Put simply, a genre world is a 'textual, social and industrial complex in which people work together to create and circulate specific types of books' (Wilkins *et al.*, 2022: 16). This framework builds on Howard S. Becker's work in *Art Worlds*, in which he argues that art is produced by a network of collective and cooperative activity, rather than by a sole individual (1982). This decentralisation of the genius figure of the author allows for an examination of the 'radiating network' or 'cast of characters' and their contributions to the production, circulation, and appreciation of art (Becker, 1982: xxiv). Extending this premise, the genre worlds model examines the 'collective activity that goes into the creation and circulation of genre texts and is particularly focused on the communities, collaborations, and industrial pressures that drive and are driven by the processes of socio-artistic formations' (Fletcher *et al.*, 2018: 998).

This literary sociological approach allows us to 'move away from the taxonomies and defenses that have dominated the field and see genre texts as the results of human creative collaboration, as the products of commercial negotiation and strategy, and as levers for social connection and engagement' (Wilkins *et al.*, 2022: 2). This relatively holistic approach to the study of genres supports our aim of mapping romance fiction in the Philippines, a large and diverse sector of the local publishing industry that is evolving at a rapid rate, as well as the forces that contribute to its evolution. As Wilkins *et al.* note, '[w]hile close and comparative reading of genre texts and their paratexts – book covers, blurbs, titles – is an important part of mapping the operations of genre worlds, so too is attending to the collaborative social and industrial networks in which genre texts arise' (2022: 16).

Wilkins *et al.* introduce this model by examining the genre worlds of romance, fantasy, and crime in Australia, but their framework is highly applicable to other local publishing territories and considers the global publishing context in which local book cultures are increasingly situated. Exploring different publishing territories through this lens highlights the locally specific ways in which genre worlds arise and the forces that contribute to the development of distinctive social, textual, and industrial characteristics. As in Australia, the Filipino romance genre world consists of unique social practices, textual conventions, and industry structures, which also interact in distinctive ways. By examining the Filipino romance industry, a key social formation in #RomanceClass, and a selection of the texts themselves, we are thus adopting a multistrand, multilayered approach to genre: one which enables us to understand not just what is in Filipino romance novels but how they are produced and received and why they are so popular.

Methods

The romance publishing industry of the Philippines is highly complex and entangled. Several organisations compete in this space, employing various business models, courting various audiences, and engaging in the production of different kinds of romance fiction, each with its own unique history. We examine several different sectors and aspects of the Filipino romance genre world in our exploration of industrial landscape, social formations, and texts. However, each of these is worthy of its own book-length study, which we do not have the capacity to do here.

Therefore, we have combined this broad look at the genre world with a case study approach. Specifically, we are using #RomanceClass, a Filipino romance self-publishing collective, as a focal point for navigating this complex landscape. They are an ideal case study for this kind of work because they are a grass-roots initiative, and many of the different practices they have adopted for navigating the Filipino romance genre world are solutions to problems this genre world has created – thus offering bigger insight into its nature as well as specific insight into the collective.

We use mixed methods, combining qualitative and quantitative and primary and secondary data, in order to capture a substantial part of our multi-site field of analysis. The data for our case study is drawn primarily from fieldwork we conducted at and around the 2019 #RomanceClass October Feels Fest event. This included eighteen in-depth semi-structured interviews with #RomanceClass community members, including authors and actors that perform at the live reading events. These were conducted in person in Manila in 2019, ranging from thirty to ninety minutes. Most interviews were conducted one-on-one but some were conducted in a small group at the request of the participants. In addition to the longer in-depth interviews, we conducted 'vox pop'–style (very brief) interviews with twelve attendees at the October Feels Fest. Some of these attendees were other authors in the community, audience members, and artists. These short interviews ranged between two and five minutes.

In addition, as part of our ethnographic case study approach, we explored physical locations of significance to the community. For example, we interviewed Mina V. Esguerra at Spiral, a restaurant at Sofitel Philippine Plaza in Pasay, Metro Manila, which featured prominently in one of her novels. We met Tania Arpa, another author, at Commune Café in Makati, where a previous live reading had been held, and our first group interview with a few other authors was conducted at The Podium, a mall in Ortigas where the first workshop with actors was held. We took ourselves on field trips to bookstores and malls to get a sense of the broader sites of book distribution and culture in the Philippines. Engaging with sites associated with the community's history was important in locating the community networks we were investigating, as well as mapping the Filipino romance book ecosystem more broadly.

Several of our #RomanceClass participants have previously been published by traditional publishers. Our interviews thus provided some data regarding the broader local romance publishing industry, as well as a broader sense of the problems it had engendered – which, as a community, #RomanceClass sought to solve, at industrial, relational, and textual levels. To develop a more detailed picture of the Filipino romance industry beyond #RomanceClass, we consulted grey literature, including industry reports and news, as well as other secondary data, including scholarship.

This Element covers a large, multilayered, and highly productive sector of the Filipino publishing industry. It explores the distinct genre histories of the different kinds of romance that have flourished in this territory and the social, political, and technological contexts that have shaped their development. It analyses the close connections forged between romance publishing and other media sectors in the Philippines and the unique reception practices that ensure the success of romance adaptations, offering a picture of a complex and distinctive genre world.

About This Element

In Chapter 1, 'The Filipino Romance Publishing Industry', we outline the industrial formation of the Filipino romance genre world and explore the field's increasing intersection with platform economies and the entertainment media industry.

Chapter 2, 'Filipino Romance Texts: From Tagalog Pocketbooks to #RomanceClass', we examine the texts themselves. Looking at two distinctive kinds of Filipino romance – Tagalog pocketbooks and English-language #RomanceClass novels – we analyse their different textual conventions and the different markets they address, and the ways in which the latter provides alternatives to the former.

Chapter 3, 'Collectivity and Care: The Case of #RomanceClass Sociality', narrows in on our case study of #RomanceClass to explore the ways social relationships shape industrial and textual practices. It examines the ways in which particular community practices emerged in reaction to or as a solution for issues engendered by the broader genre world, demonstrating the key role of sociality in publishing ecosystems.

1 The Filipino Romance Publishing Industry

The Philippines has a distinctive and thriving romance publishing industry that has evolved in response to the country's economic and socio-political history. It is an industry structured by national languages (Filipino and English), disparate publishing models, and integrated digital technologies. Tagalog/Taglish romance fiction has been a local powerhouse since its introduction in the mid-1980s and remains a dominant and bestselling part of the Filipino publishing industry. In the early twenty-first century, several new competitors have worked to address other shares of the Filipino romance market. In the early 2000s, the development of English-language romance lines by conglomerate publishers sought to capture Class A–C readers. More recently, digital platform companies such as Wattpad have successfully integrated themselves into production and reception processes in the local publishing industry, contributing to the development of a highly productive YA romance fiction sector.

Romance publishing is closely connected to other media industries in the Philippines. Here, adaptations of romance fiction are driven by the nation's highly concentrated media ownership, commercial partnerships, and distinctive Filipino reception practices among audiences. The productive links developed between publishing, platform, and media companies in the Philippines aid in more efficient acquisition and distribution processes while also creating a highly competitive landscape for authors and books. The concentration of media ownership, in addition to emerging corporate partnerships between publishers and media producers, has resulted in an ecosystem in which the publishing and entertainment media sectors are closely intertwined.

This chapter introduces the landscape of the Filipino romance publishing industry. It maps the histories and productive modes of four distinctive sectors of the romance publishing industry in the Philippines: Tagalog pocketbook romance, English chick lit romance, YA romance by platform publishers, and self-published English-language romance published by #RomanceClass. Here, we outline the major publishers and socio-political structures that have shaped the evolution of the industry and which underpin the specific textual evolutions and social relationships explored in the following two chapters.

1.1 Traditional Romance Publishers: From Tagalog Pocketbooks to English-Language Chick Lit

In 1986, Books for Pleasure published its first set of locally produced Tagalog romance pocketbooks under its Valentine Romances imprint. Previously, Books for Pleasure had been not a publisher but a distributor: it had served as the local representative for several British and American publishers since 1976, including romance publishers Mills & Boon and Bantam Books (Jurilla, 2008). The political and economic conditions of the Philippines under the dictatorship of President Ferdinand E. Marcos forced local publishers and book traders in the Philippines to develop new revenues to survive. According to Jurilla, the 'steady inflation forced many local businesses to cut back drastically if not shut down completely', and several publishers resorted to the printing of office stationery, maps, recipe books, and calendars (2008: 163). During this period of economic diversification among local businesses, Books for Pleasure shifted from being a distributor of imported books to publishing original Filipino fiction. Locally published Filipino romance fiction, more commonly known as Tagalog pocketbooks, emerged within this political and economic context.

Tagalog pocketbook romances are short, category-length romance novels written primarily in Taglish, a hybrid between Tagalog/Filipino and English (for more on their use of language, see Chapter 2). They have historically followed a general formula, in terms of both narrative structure and publication format. As Jurilla describes:

> Each volume is published as part of a series. All are printed as paperbacks with glossy covers and newsprint leaves, and sized in 'pocketbook' format, typically measuring 17 x 10.5 cm and consisting of 128 pages ... They are sold at a price ranging from twenty to forty pesos per copy, cheaper than a fast food meal from any of the popular chains all over the country. In a sense, the books are local versions of foreign romance novels of the Mills & Boon or Harlequin Romances variety. (2008: 161)

While pocketbook romances were influenced in part by Mills & Boon English-language category romances, which were imported to the Philippines in the mid-twentieth century (including by Books for Pleasure) and read primarily by upper-class Filipinos, pocketbook romances were produced to be sold in supermarkets to a primary readership of women from low-middle and high-lower classes (Jurilla, 2008). As will be explored in the next chapter, this market audience informed the kinds of narrative that dominated Tagalog romances. These novels unsurprisingly focus on a central love story and 'the ideal that "love conquers all"', and they are 'unabashedly melodramatic and steadfastly formulaic in nature' (Jurilla, 2008: 161).

The inaugural four Valentine Romances Tagalog pocketbook titles were launched in 1986. The initial launch was delayed by a year due to the 1985 presidential election and subsequent protests. The titles – *Bawal Kitang Ibigin* (I Am Forbidden to Love You) by Helen Meriz (1985), *Kahit Mahal Kita* (Even if I Love You) by Maria Elena Cruz (1985), *Pag-ibig Ko, Karapatan Ko* (My Love, My Right) by Lualhati Bautista (1985), and *Laro ng Mga Puso* (Game of Hearts) by Marissa Pascual (1985) – each had an initial print run of 3,000 copies. Subsequent releases came slowly and intermittently as Books for Pleasure established itself and gradually sourced new authors and manuscripts. The first four Valentine Romances books went through a second, and sometimes third, print run as the books quickly sold out and demand grew (Buhain, 1998), demonstrating their immediate popularity and success. According to Benjamin Ocampo, publisher of Books of Pleasure, the print runs of Valentine Romances titles quickly grew to 5,000, 6,000, 8,000, and then 10,000 copies per title (Jurilla, 2008). These figures are significant in demonstrating the performance of these books in the Filipino market: as Jurilla notes, '[i]n the Philippines, a book's performance in the market is usually gauged by how many copies were printed and how many impressions or editions were issued rather than how many copies were actually sold' (2008: 15). In 1988, Books for Pleasure engaged the services of the book distribution company Megastrat, enabling the nationwide distribution of Valentine Romances titles and spurring the popularity of pocketbook romances across the provinces.

In the early 1990s, other Philippine publishers began carving out their share of the Tagalog romance fiction market. These publishers included Bookware, Anvil Publishing (a local trade publisher) with their Rosas imprint, Salesiana Publishing (a religious publisher), De La Salle University Press (a university press), and Atlas Publishing (primarily a comic book, magazine, and textbook publisher), among others. These publishers adopted different strategies in an attempt to cement their share in the Filipino romance market, with varying degrees of success. In 1992, Precious Pages Corporation was set up by Segundo Matias Jr and Richard Reynante, freelance writers for television at the time, with the sole purpose of publishing romance fiction under its Precious Hearts Romances imprint (Buhain, 1998). Books published by Precious Hearts closely followed the narrative structure of the titles popularised by Books for Pleasure. While they began publishing just one book per month, their list quickly grew to around twenty-five new titles per month by the late 1990s. As the books gained popularity, new writers were signed, and the company invested in their own production and printing technologies. Anvil's Rosas books, conversely, were 'packaged, priced, promoted, and distributed in exactly the same way as the Valentine [Romances] line was' but did not follow the same narrative formula that had been so successful in the Books for Pleasure titles (Jurilla, 2008: 168). Instead, Anvil acquired romance manuscripts from authors of literary fiction who infused their manuscripts with themes such as 'rape, incest, discrimination and violence against women, mail-order brides, prostitution, poverty, and environmental degradation' and did not end their stories with happily-ever-afters (HEAs), a convention of genre romance (Jurilla, 2008: 168). De La Salle University Press took a similar approach, attempting to take advantage of the popularity of Tagalog romances but with a more literary bent. This approach misunderstood the conventions and reader expectations of the romance, a genre that is intensively market driven. De La Salle University Press discontinued their line of 'literary' Tagalog romances soon after launch and Anvil Publishing, despite having direct access to the vast retail network of National Bookstore, discontinued their Rosas line after producing only thirty titles (Raymundo, 2004).

By the mid-1990s, there were thirty-five Filipino romance novel series in circulation, produced by twenty-three publishers (Jurilla, 2008). However, publishers such as Books for Pleasure and Precious Pages found continued success by being attuned to market expectations. Their books were priced to be accessible for a broad socio-economic audience, packaged with familiar paratext, and featured reliable narratives. By 1997, Precious Hearts had published around 400 Filipino romance novels, launched six other romance fiction imprints, and had become the biggest and most successful publisher of Tagalog romance fiction (Jurilla, 2008). Since 2011, Precious Pages has published approximately fifty titles per month across Precious Hearts and other imprints and remains the dominant publisher of Tagalog pocketbook romances (Precious Hearts Romance, 2016; France-Presse, 2011).

Tagalog romances were bestsellers in the late twentieth century and dominated the Philippine romance fiction industry virtually unchallenged until the turn of the century. They remain popular; however, the 2000s saw the emergence of local English-language romance fiction, which, as will be discussed further in Chapter 2, spoke primarily to a different section of the market (Classes A–C, i.e. those who had acquired an education level that allowed them mastery of the colonial language English). In 2002, Summit Media, a privately owned magazine publishing company, established Summit Books and published the first English-language chick lit novel. A short book, *Getting Better* by Tara F. T. Sering (2002), was distributed as a free copy with the purchase of *Cosmopolitan Philippines*. *Cosmopolitan Philippines* is also owned by Summit Media, and Sering was, at the time, the magazine's Managing Editor. *Getting Better* was published as market research: within the issue of *Cosmopolitan* was a survey asking if readers would like to see more books like *Getting Better*. The results of the survey were positive, so by early 2003, four more chick lit titles were published by Summit Books: *Drama Queen* by Abi Aquino, *The Breakup Diaries* by Maya Calica, *Mr. Write* by M. D. Balangue, and *Almost Married* by Sering, the sequel to *Getting Better*. Globally, chick lit and romantic comedies were widely popular across media forms, including, for instance, Helen Fielding's *Bridget Jones's Diary* (1996). The subsequent Summit Books chick lit titles were published under the Modern Fiction imprint, with Sering acting as publisher. Mina V. Esguerra, who began publishing for Summit Books in 2009, described the books published under the Modern Fiction imprint as 'very *Bridget Jones*, but Philippine' (interview). Summit

Books and its Modern Fiction line repopularised English-language romance in the Philippines, more than twenty years after Books for Pleasure stopped importing UK-published Mills & Boon.

The development of English-language romance in the Philippines was underpinned by processes of globalisation and transnationalism. The initiation of Summit Books' English-language romance novels is fundamentally tied to conglomeration and the licensed importation of *Cosmopolitan* by Summit Media, which worked to develop a market for transnational media products marketed to women. The success of these titles is also linked to the postcolonial attitudes of post-war Philippines, which prized Westernised titles by foreign authors across genres (Santiago, 2009). These transnationalist politics primarily played out in Summit Books titles through dynamics of language and class. While both Filipino and English are official national languages in the Philippines, English was practically the sole language of instruction in educational settings between 1901 and 1974 (Tupas & Lorente, 2014) and is the primary language of commerce, politics, and law.

Summit Books titles targeted the middle-class readers of *Cosmopolitan Philippines* magazine and were influenced by the post-feminist discourse of sex and gender promoted in the magazine's coverage. Informed by global and local feminisms, these novels worked to subvert stereotypical representations of Filipina women, who have traditionally been portrayed in Filipino media as:

> the innocent and virginal girl; the virtuous, self-negating woman; the silent, suffering wife and mother; the faithful and constantly-waiting sweetheart; the dutiful sister or daughter; and the benevolent aunt who chooses single-blessedness for familial duties ... On the negative side of the spectrum we have the images of the fallen woman, the insufferable nag, the angry bitch, the seductive temptress, the despicable whore, and the frigid spinster. (Evasco, 2002: 167)

Sering and the other Summit Books authors in the early 2000s disrupted these images of Filipina women by highlighting the independence and agency of their main characters, within the context of romantic love and heterosexual relationships. The progressivism of the chick lit titles published by Summit Books at this time was also delimited by class. Reflecting their middle-class target market, the novels featured characters who, as Katrina Stuart Santiago summarised, 'locate themselves in the Philippines, in the Makati and Ortigas business districts, in the gimmick places of Malate, Makati, Libis, and Boracay, in the condominiums and apartments that have risen in the metropolis' (2009: 72). Politics of language, class, gender, and sex are intricately interwoven within the narratives of these novels and reflect the complexity of the national book industry. It is, in many ways, fragmented, with different sections of the romance publishing industry speaking to segments of the market without a lot of overlap. This means that the texts reflect significantly different priorities, as will be discussed further in Chapter 2.

1.2 Platformed Publishing in the Philippines

Digital platforms have radically transformed the Filipino publishing industry in the early twenty-first century. In particular, Summit Media's Pop Fiction platform and the Toronto-based Wattpad platform have restructured processes of creation, production, and dissemination in the Philippines. The typical internet usage practices of Filipino people shed some light on why digital publishing platforms have been so popular and contributed to their successful integration into the publishing and media industries in the Philippines. While internet adoption in the Philippines is only just above the worldwide average (68 per cent and 62.5 per cent of the population, respectively), Filipinos who are connected to the Internet are avid users (We Are Social, 2022). The average daily time spent on the Internet by Filipino users between 16 and 64 years old is 10 hours and 27 minutes (We Are Social, 2022), well above the worldwide average of 6 hours and 58 minutes. Filipinos are also first in the world in watching content via streaming services: 98.3 per cent of the population compared to 93.5 per cent of the worldwide population. Data reported by Wattpad shows that Filipinos' access to online entertainment is not limited to content streaming. As of 2018, seven million Filipinos access Wattpad each month, making it the second largest market for Wattpad after the United

States (Adobo Magazine, 2018). This usage data demonstrates the connect-edness of Filipinos to the Internet and their propensity to access entertain-ment online, which demonstrates why Wattpad has invested in partnerships and adaptations in the Philippines that leverage this popularity.

Since the early 2010s, Philippine publishers and media producers have been investing in digital platforms to find, source, and develop content. Summit Books launched its Pop Fiction imprint in 2013, sourcing many of its original titles from CandyMag.com, the proprietary online site for Summit Media's *Candy* magazine, somewhat mirroring the successful horizontal integration approach of its Cosmopolitan and Modern Fiction imprint. The first title published in connection to the Pop Fiction imprint was *She's Dating the Gangster* by Bianca Bernardino (2013). Bernardino first published this title as serialised fiction on CandyMag.com's TeenTalk section before cross-posting it to Wattpad, where it amassed a large online reader base. Despite the initial scepticism that consumers would be willing to purchase print books that they could read online for free, the online popularity of *She's Dating the Gangster* was mirrored by the title's print sales. A month after its release, *She's Dating the Gangster* reached the top of National Book Store's Philippine bestseller list. Perhaps due to the success of Bernardino's book as well as convenience, many of the imprint's original titles were sourced from the CandyMag TeenTalk forum. Summit Media also launched PopFictionBooks.com, a site that originally served as an online catalogue of books published by Pop Fiction but has quickly evolved to be a social media platform for authors, artists, and readers, where members can access free stories, read relevant articles, and see updates from their favourite authors and artists, as well as send manuscripts directly to editors.

The rise of these local platforms is tied to the success of global ones: in particular, Wattpad. This Toronto-based multiplatform entertainment social media company, which launched in 2007, has had a particularly dramatic impact on the Filipino publishing and entertainment industries (Parnell, 2022). Since around 2013, Wattpad has developed business part-nerships with local publishers and film and TV production companies to source and adapt popular content from the platform. Wattpad, which presents read data on stories and authors, serves as a useful resource for publishers to determine trends in publishing, as well as to discover new and popular authors among the young readers that comprise Wattpad's primary user demographic. Indeed, the selling power of Wattpad-sourced titles in the Philippines may be attributed to the popularity of the platform among young Filipino readers. Wattpad established its first formal partnership in the Philippines in 2014 with Pop Fiction, which enabled Wattpad a share in the editorial control and profits of published texts sourced from its platform (Wattpad, 2014). The partnership between Wattpad and Pop Fiction marked the beginning of the platform's eventual prominence in the publishing and media industries of the Philippines. In 2014, major national production companies, including Viva Films, TV5, and ABS-CBN, began adapting Wattpad stories into films and television series. Many of these were in the genre of teleseryes, or Filipino telenovelas or P-dramas, and nearly all were teen fiction and/or romance. Wattpad offers local publishers and producers data-driven popularity metrics based on the platform's extensive data collection of writing and reading practices of its global user base: something that mirrors and extends the tried-and-tested logic that underpins the adaptation industry (Ellis, 1982; Murray, 2012; Parnell, 2021). Wattpad's impact on the local publishing lists extends beyond its formal partnerships: large book publishers such as Psicom Publishing have been using the direct messaging function on the platform to approach Wattpad authors and license their work since the early 2010s.

In 2019, Wattpad partnered with Anvil Publishing to create Bliss Books, a dedicated YA imprint that publishes popular stories from the platform. Books published by Bliss Books combine elements of Tagalog pocketbook romances, such as the use of Taglish, but adapt them for their globalised, digital native young reader market. The brand power of Wattpad in the local book market is emphasised through the paratextual alignment of Bliss Books covers with the platform. Authors' Wattpad usernames are featured prominently, often to the exclusion of their real names, and the Bliss Books logo, positioned in the top right-hand corner of covers, features the distinctive Wattpad orange brand colour. This branded orange – titled Hero Orange – is often also used as a border around the cover image (Parnell, 2022). These paratextual elements highlight the importance of authors' Wattpad followings in the Filipino book market and the way in which notoriety and popularity online are believed to influence book sales.

The cross-media promotional power of platform authors in the Philippine publishing landscape is exemplified by Jonahmae Pacala (@Jonaxx on Wattpad and her book covers). With more than 5.1 million followers globally, Filipino author Jonaxx is the most followed author on Wattpad and, as of the time of writing in 2022, every story she has published on Wattpad has read counts in the millions, ranging from around 18 million to 146 million (Jonaxx, 2022). This popularity has generated success in the publishing industry beyond the platform. In 2014, she began publishing some of her titles under Summit Books' Pop Fiction and Sizzle imprints (Pop Fiction, 2020). In 2017, Summit Books launched Majesty Press (MPress), an imprint dedicated to publishing unabridged and uncut versions of titles by Jonaxx (Summit Books, 2017). Jonaxx's success as a platform author highlights the increasing power of Wattpad and other platforms to facilitate the development of creators, audiences, and markets.

1.3 Romance Fiction in the Filipino Adaptation Industry

The romance publishing industry in the Philippines is especially notable in its close connection with other media sectors. Traditional publishers, Wattpad and other platform companies, as well as the self-publishing collective #RomanceClass, all contribute to a highly active romance adaptation industry in the Philippines. Several Tagalog and Wattpad romance stories have been adapted by local film producers, television series, and streaming platforms.

The adaptation industry of the Philippines is buttressed in part by the organisational structures of several traditional publishing houses. The major traditional publishers in the Philippines, including Summit Books, Anvil Publishing, and Psicom, operate as subsidiaries of large media or retail conglomerates. Summit Books was established in 2002 by Summit Media, a privately owned media conglomerate that began as a consumer magazine publisher in 1995. As has been described above, the operations and outputs of Summit Books are closely connected to the media properties of Summit Media. Summit Books was originally established in collaboration with *Cosmopolitan Philippines*, and Pop Fiction – Summit Books' most popular imprint for teen fiction, romance, and genre fiction – has sourced many of its authors from the online forums (for example, Teen Talk and Creative Corner) associated with Summit Media's *Candy* magazine. Anvil Publishing was founded in 1990 as the book publishing arm of the National Book Store, a national bookseller that was established in 1942 and is now the largest chain book retailer in the Philippines. Viva-Psicom, a large publishing house that began publishing chick lit and contemporary romance in the early 2000s, is owned by Viva Communications Inc. Founded in 1981, Viva Communications now owns a further two publishing houses alongside several film, television, and music subsidiaries (including as the licensed distributor for many international products such as Nickelodeon, 20th Century Fox, and Disney) where its influence on the Filipino media culture has been most acute. These large publishing companies benefit from extensive distribution systems as well as human and economic resources associated with conglomeration.

The interconnectedness of the publishing and media industries in the Philippines has led to several cross-media romance adaptations. *She's Dating the Gangster* by Bianca Bernardino is a key example of the success of adapted romance fiction titles across Filipino media organisations. In 2014, a year after it was published by Pop Fiction, *She's Dating the Gangster* was released as a film by ABS-CBN Film Productions Inc. after the title proved its popularity on Summit Media's CandyMag.com TeenTalk forum, Wattpad, and in print sales. The film, which secured more than PHP 260 million at the box office, starred Kathryn Barnardo and Daniel Padilla, aka the love team KathNiel (Philippine Entertainment Portal, 2014).

Romance adaptations in the Philippines are primarily produced through partnerships brokered between publishers and broadcast networks. Two significant romance adaptation TV programmes are *Precious Hearts Romances Presents* and *Wattpad Presents*. Beginning in May 2009, ABS-CBN, one of two conglomerates that operated as a duopoly (alongside GMA) and which had the largest audience share nationwide in 2019 (ABS-CBN, 2020), broadcast *Precious Hearts Romances Presents*, a series that adapted bestselling paperbacks by Precious Hearts Romances (i.e. Tagalog pocketbook romances). This series ran five days a week for just over a decade, ending in September 2019, and is the longest-running romance adaptation series in the country. In 2014, after building successful deals with book publishers, Wattpad partnered with the local network TV5 to produce *Wattpad Presents*. This weekly series featured teen fiction and romance stories, which originally unfolded over multiple episodes but eventually developed to contain entire Filipino Wattpad stories in standalone episodes. According to the platform, *Wattpad Presents* aired approximately 265 episodes in its first two years, comprising nearly 65 original Wattpad stories, and reached an average audience of 1.6 million per episode (Wattpad, 2016). Many Wattpad authors of stories adapted for *Wattpad Presents* had already been republished by the Life Is Beautiful (LIB) publishing company or were subsequently offered deals by traditional publishers. In doing so, traditional publishers and Wattpad capitalised on the sales fillip often seen with cross-media texts in the adaptation industry (Murray, 2012).

In 2020, when the Duterte government refused to renew ABS-CBN's broadcast licence, the conglomerate shifted to producing and disseminating adaptations of romance novels sourced from Wattpad and LIB through iWantTFC, a streaming platform it owns. For example, *He's Into Her*, a Philippine teen romantic comedy television series based on the 2013 novel of the same name by Maxinejiji (Maxine Lat Calibuso), was released in 2021, starring Donny Pangilinan and Belle Mariano, aka the love team DonBelle (Dumaual, 2021). Wattpad has developed partnerships with television networks and streaming platforms globally, including Netflix, Hulu, Sony (US), Huayi Brothers (South Korea), iFlix (Indonesia), and eOne (Canada). Wattpad's partnership with TV5, however, represents the most closely integrated relationship in the entertainment media sphere. As with its partnership with Anvil Publishing and Bliss Books, Wattpad has greater curatorial input into the stories adapted for *Wattpad Presents*.

What makes Wattpad's integration into entertainment media in the Philippines so successful is the industry's long history of innovation and development. The television industry in the Philippines has not experienced the disruptions or audience fragmentation propelled by digital technologies to the same extent as other markets. Rather, digital and mobile technologies have largely supported the industry as Filipino 'television producers have been very successful in reintegrating successful content from new media platforms into traditionally broadcast programmes' (Pertierra, 2021: 70). Young Filipino audiences have followed and supported this reintegration. Television in the Philippines has also long been a 'national conveyor of popular culture and entertainment' that includes romance and romantic elements (Pertierra, 2021: 70). For example, *Eat Bulaga!*, a hugely popular Philippine television noontime variety show broadcast by GMA Network, featured a live soap opera parody segment, *Kalyeserye* (a portmanteau for *Kalye* 'street' and *serye* 'series') that drew on elements of romantic comedy, drama, and reality television. This mini-show evolved to focus on the fictional romance between Alden Richards and Maine Mendoza's 'Yaya Dub' (commonly referred to together as AlDub, another love team). With Richards usually based in the *Eat Bulaga!* studio and Mendoza travelling around to different external locations, the fictional romance between this love team has developed through distanced interactions on the show's split-screen frame, primarily by lip-syncing to pop songs and movie audio clips, as well as written messages on posters. After running for a year and a half, and for 400 episodes with an initial runtime of a few minutes then expanding to over half an hour each, the segment ended in December 2016. As Soledad S. Reyes puts it,

> AlDub has become a certified success among millions not because it stands out in the midst of similar shows (perhaps it does in terms of its difference with Showtime or Wowowee) . . . in the show we find the crystallisation of the nation's major literary and cultural traditions. (2015)

AlDub is emblematic of several forces in the Philippine media and popular culture that make adaptations of romance novels successful. These include the popularity of television as the most used and trusted medium in the Philippines (Estella & Löffelholz, n.d.) and – as have been mentioned several times already – love teams (Bolisay, 2015).

Love teams are a unique feature of the Filipino cultural industries, and they contribute to the successful adaptation of romance texts in the Philippines. They are considered to be a 'Pinoy (shortened version of Filipino) invention', and refer to the pairing of mostly heterosexual couples whose projects in the world of show business always involve each other (Santiago, 2018: 1). This consistent selling of the imaginary couple as a romance commodity oftentimes results in the audience hoping that a real romance between them will blossom (Bolisay, 2015). The formation of Filipino love teams by studios dates to the silent film era of the 1920s–1930s. Today, contemporary love teams are heavily mediated and social media is a key site in which audiences engage with and constantly reproduce their personas. In a kind of feedback loop, love teams – like Alden Richards and Maine Mendoza (AlDub), Donny Pangilinan and Belle Mariano (DonBelle), and Kathryn Barnardo and Daniel Padilla (KathNiel) – have become central to the user experience of many Filipino Wattpad readers and writers. #KathNiel, for example, was the most-searched term on Wattpad in the Philippines in 2016, demonstrating the way young Filipino audiences engage with romantic texts and characters across media (Anderson, 2016a). In other words, young romance audiences in the Philippines will follow their favourite stories, authors, and actors across media products, platforms, and media spaces.

Romance book publishing in the Philippines exists within a complex and highly interconnected multimedia sphere. The close connection between romance fiction publishing and other media in the Philippines in the early twenty-first century, through adaptations, marketing, and love teams, is an important evolution in the Filipino history of the book. By the 2020s, the romance fiction book industry in the Philippines is most legible when it is conceived of as another (important) node in the media sphere.

1.4 #RomanceClass: A Self-Published Romance Community

#RomanceClass, the self-publishing collective which forms the central case study of this Element, was established in 2013 by author Mina V. Esguerra and has developed in response to the publishing and media landscape described above. Indeed, while the community has distinct priorities and a clear ethos, many facets of its development can be conceived of as solutions to problems posed by this landscape. For instance, founder Esguerra had been publishing in Summit Books' Modern Fiction line since 2009. At this time, the imprint was releasing approximately three or four titles per year – 'if we're lucky', Esguerra said (interview) – compared to hundreds of Tagalog romances. Esguerra stated, 'if I wrote more than one book, I had to wait a year or two for them to even consider it because they had other authors' (interview). On top of this, the impact of Wattpad on the local publishing industry was acutely felt by Esguerra and the other early #RomanceClass authors. As Esguerra stated,

> the reason why I feel that chick-lit contemporary romance in English was slowing down in the Philippines was they had instant hits [from Wattpad] . . . I mean, they were using the same team, I mean the team that used to work with me would work on these Wattpad books, release a new one every month and get times 7, times 10, times 20 – the sales. (Interview)

The limited opportunities provided by Summit Books' English-language romance publishing schedule, despite the popularity of the imprint's books, prompted Esguerra to become a hybrid author, self-publishing alongside publishing through traditional houses.

#RomanceClass began as a free online class run by Esguerra that taught authors how to write romance fiction. The class began as a private Facebook group that originally had around 100 people, including 'people who had interacted with [Esguerra] as readers for years' that she knew 'were interested in writing and maybe just needed a deadline and an incentive' (interview). Class materials and activities varied widely: Esguerra would post lecture videos on topics related to romance fiction,

> and then people would comment, and discuss, and ask questions, and then there would be a deadline. At the beginning of the class, I would give them a schedule . . . [and activities such as] you pitch your story as if it's a back cover blurb or an Amazon description and people will react, like 'Will I buy this? Is this something interesting to me?' So that, and then an outline because I advocated for outlining, so outline, from beginning to end. Next was outline, next

> was act one, so I mean, I'm not checking everyone's writing
> but just reminding people that if you want to finish on time,
> you have to be done with your first act, third by this date,
> and then act two, and then final. (Interview)

The first course ran for six months, but as many of the original authors finished well before the deadline, Esguerra ran subsequent courses for around three months. In the first course, Esguerra recalls, 'maybe about 50 were really active, like participating and the others were lurking, and then, at the end of six months, [there were] 16 finished manuscripts' (interview). Esguerra drew on her traditional publishing network and attempted to get local publishers interested in the sixteen finished contemporary romance novels from the class.

The tightly networked publishing landscape and limited publishing opportunities impelled the community to adapt, and the class evolved into what Esguerra defined as a 'self-publishing support group' (interview). Now, #RomanceClass operates somewhere between a self-publishing collective and a micro-publisher. As will be discussed further in Chapter 3, members of the community participate in different, and sometimes overlapping, publishing roles: author, editor, cover designer, marketing, and so on. While books published through this network share the #RomanceClass colophon, marking them as #RomanceClass books, there is no commissioning editor and minimal gatekeeping within the community beyond the requirements that the books must be genre romance (i.e. end with a happy-ever-after) and must have been worked on by at least two #RomanceClass members.

In terms of printing and distribution, #RomanceClass authors operate similarly to other self-published authors globally. They use a local print-on-demand printer to create their paperbacks and self-publishing platforms, such as Amazon Kindle Direct Publishing, to produce their e-books. They sell their books through the #RomanceClass website, maintained by community member Miles Tan, as well as other e-bookstores (Amazon, Kobo, and Apple Books, for example). Their live reading events have also provided them with a more romance-friendly space to sell their print books. Before their first live reading event (an April Feels Day), a few community members had attended and taken 'out the table' at a 'local indie fair . . . that had everybody, like comic artists, the edgier indie stuff, zines, stickers, stuff like that', but had felt uncomfortable with the attitudes of the general readers in attendance (Esguerra, interview). As Esguerra added,

> And when there were a lot of guys, it was a weird dynamic when we were at the table because they don't like stopping at your table and we were wondering . . . I don't know, they were not comfortable stopping and picking up and looking at the books . . .. And then it got to a point where there was a guy who was just hovering, like he dropped by three times, hovering without picking anything up and we didn't know if he genuinely was interested but had all this internal crisis whatever that he couldn't but we thought, you know, we shouldn't be in a place where people felt that way.
>
> So, immediately after the fair we were in the restaurant, and we were planning, like we should make something – that's just us and that was . . . we did that in Feb and then April of that year, we did our first April Feels day . . .. We rented out a waffle place, a waffle shop, [a] cute waffle shop . . . there were five live readers; we would sell and they would read and 80 people showed up. (Interview)

The handselling method at the live readings has developed over the years. Recently, Tan, who manages the community's website, put together a barcode system for books. Before, authors selling books at the live readings would 'manually list book purchases' but now sales per author are automated (Esguerra, interview).

This community operates with increasingly professionalised practices and has developed explicitly from traditionally published English-language Filipino romance. Indeed, several #RomanceClass authors began their writing and publishing careers with Summit Books and other English-language romance publishers in the early 2000s. Despite the global influences that contributed to the formation of Summit Books, including

Cosmopolitan and UK and US chick lit, #RomanceClass is significantly more closely connected to the dominant US publishing industry. They take their definition of romance fiction largely from the Romance Writers of America (RWA), the longest-running romance fiction industry organisation, which defines romance genre fiction as containing two essential elements: a central love story and an emotionally satisfying and optimistic ending (RWA, n.d.). While #RomanceClass authors actively and intentionally write with Filipino readers in mind and prioritise Filipino representation, including on the covers, they are highly aware of the global romance industry. This global (and globalised) outlook reveals itself through the community's engagement with romance writers in other countries (primarily the USA) and their inclusion of characters who are part of the Filipino American diaspora, an otherwise under-represented group in Filipino romance fiction. Engaging with the hegemonic US romance community has contributed to their visibility globally. #RomanceClass books are sometimes included in book lists by US-based publications of diverse and inclusive titles. Carla de Guzman has two books – *Sweet on You* (2020) and *A Match Made in Lipa* (2022) – published with large US romance publisher Carina Press. The connections they have forged with the dominant US romance industry are intricately tied to the community's use of English as a primary language. By virtue of fluency, romance authors and readers from dominant English-language publishing territories can more readily engage with #RomanceClass titles. The visibility of this community globally is also largely driven by active networking by several central figures in the community, including Esguerra, and their strategic use of social media platforms.

While #RomanceClass is a highly professionalised network involved in the production of books, it emphasises social collectivity and relationships within the community. These social relationships are made and reinforced through communication channels as well as the biannual live reading events – April Feels Day and October Feels Fest – the community holds. At these live reading events, members of the community, including authors, editors, and readers, gather to watch local actors read curated passages from romance novels by the community's authors. Because of the dual-perspective narrative of most #RomanceClass books, these live readings often feature two actors portraying the two protagonists. This format has encouraged the development of a grass-roots form of love teams within the community. Perhaps the most popular #RomanceClass live reading team, based on our ethnographic, social media, and interview data, is Gio Gahol and Rachel Coates (commonly referred to as #gahoates on Twitter and Instagram). #Gahoates is a kind of funhouse mirror reflection of Filipino love teams in that the pair do not map straightforwardly onto the construct: they are not manufactured by a studio marketing team but have evolved from repeat performances as an audience favourite (Parnell *et al.*, 2021a). Further, while the community seems to love the #gahoates pairing, they do not believe or promote the idea that Gahol and Coates are a couple in real life and are equally thrilled to see them perform with other actors. Popular live reading pairs like Gahol and Coates and performers like Sam Aquino and Jef Flores are often featured in the marketing material of #RomanceClass for live reading events and in other media, including community-produced podcasts, book trailers, and audiobooks.

#RomanceClass has also continuously experimented with adaptations in several formats and the community has produced cross-media products as part of their community-building practices. As a grass-roots publishing collective, #RomanceClass has capitalised on the multimedia habits of Filipino consumers, experimenting with adaptation and transmedia story-telling across various in-person and online media formats, including holding regular live reading events with local actors (Parnell *et al.*, 2021a) and producing audio and video content on social media (Parnell *et al.*, 2021b). Since 2015, #RomanceClass has produced a podcast that comprises episodes where an actor or actors read a romance novel by a community author and author interviews. The episodes that feature readings from novels are reflective of the live reading events the community holds biannually. #RomanceClass continued to innovate with media formats during the Covid-19 pandemic lockdowns in the Philippines through transmedia products (Parnell *et al.*, 2021b). Along with many arts and cultural organisations around the world, #RomanceClass turned to online platforms to continue their events and community engagement during Covid-19. Many of the online media activities #RomanceClass produced during the pandemic were inspired by media genres popularised in other countries, reflecting the popularity and engagement in transcultural media in the Philippines. In 2020, #RomanceClass produced several new web series, posted to YouTube and streamed via Twitch, including *Mukbang Nights* and *Hello, Ever After*. *Mukbang* is a South Korean internet phenomenon that has become popular worldwide, wherein a host consumes a large amount of food while interacting with their audience in an online audio-visual broadcast (Anjani *et al.*, 2020). #RomanceClass adapted this genre by producing videos in which a few members of #RomanceClass would eat food and discuss their books. Food is a beloved part of both #RomanceClass events and books ('there's lots of food, always. At some point someone always describes what the characters are eating. No exceptions', author Carla de Guzman told us when we interviewed her in 2019), and so their adoption of mukbang shows the ways in which their 2020 digital events sought to recreate established forms of communal cohesion in a virtual co-presence space.

They also produced the *Hello, Ever After* web series, which adapted their in-person live reading events and drew on the growing popularity of born-digital fictional web series in Southeast Asia, such as Thailand's *Boys' Love* videos. While traditional television programming in the Philippines has been largely characterised by profitable nationalistic popular content, Filipino audiences are also very receptive to transcultural popular media. Other Filipino digital media creators have adapted the Japanese and Thai *Boys' Love* genre to create their own *Pinoy Boys' Love* videos on YouTube and on creative writing platforms (Fermin, 2013; Parnell *et al.*, 2021b) as well as actively engaging in transcultural online spaces and media, including Japanese anime and manga (Santos, 2019) and Korean drama (K-drama) communities (Kim, 2016). Unlike the community's live reading events, which featured actors reading passages from already-published books, *Hello, Ever After* featured original short scripts written by #RomanceClass authors. These scripts took established characters from these authors' novels and served as epilogues, where viewers could see how these characters and their romances fared during the pandemic. The scenes were purposefully written as video chats, which not only allowed for the fact that the actors were unable to physically interact with each other because of the lockdowns but also tapped into the Zoom communication aesthetic that commandeered many people's personal and professional communications during Covid-19 restrictions. Although the web series used a different video conferencing technology, community member Tania Arpa, who directed the web series episodes, adapted the nameplate feature that displayed the characters' names to align with the Zoom format more closely, demonstrating #RomanceClass's close attentiveness to developments in the global media environment as well as their dynamic creation of transmedia products rather than only adaptations. As an independent, born-digital literary organisation, #RomanceClass was able to adapt swiftly and effectively to online-only events in response to the harshness of the Filipino lockdown, creating new forms of artistic innovation by adopting the aesthetics of Zoom in their creative practice.

As a dynamic grass-roots community, #RomanceClass is well-equipped to effectively adapt to the ever-changing Philippine publishing industry. With their strong community identity and relationships, its authors produce high-quality romance that competes in the global romance genre world while they actively and continuously develop their local audience, putting them in a somewhat unique position in the complex transmedia landscape of the Filipino romance industry.

1.5 Conclusion

There are four distinct sectors of the romance industry in the Philippines: Tagalog pocketbooks, traditionally published English-language romance, platform-produced YA romance, and self-published English-language romance produced in connection with #RomanceClass. These sectors are interconnected to different levels: platform-produced YA romance is published in Taglish (a code-mixing dialect of Tagalog and English) and shares strong similarities with the Tagalog pocketbook romances, and #RomanceClass has developed on the texts introduced by traditional publishers when it comes to English-language romance fiction. Together, they represent a large and dynamic romance fiction industry in the Philippines.

Each of these sectors is also connected to the media industry and sites of bookish reception in the Philippines in distinctive ways. Media conglomeration connects many traditional publishers, from Tagalog to English romances, to film and television companies and booksellers. Anvil Publishing, for instance, is the publishing arm of National Book Store, the country's largest book retail chain, while Summit Books is associated with the Pop Fiction platform and Summit Media, which aids in the acquisition and adaptation of romance texts. In recent years, global digital writing and reading platform Wattpad has leveraged its large Filipino userbase to develop partnerships with local publishers and media companies, including Anvil Publishing and broadcast network TV5. Against this competitive and dynamic multimedia sphere, #RomanceClass has engaged in the production and development of several entertainment media texts, including audiobooks, podcasts, web series, and its biannual live reading events.

In her book history study of the Philippines, Jurilla describes the Filipino romance publishing landscape of 1985 to 2000 as 'a massive enterprise involving numerous titles issued every month ... print runs of 5,000 to 20,000 copies per title, and brief periods in which the titles sold out (some in as short as two weeks)' (2008: 184). The romance publishing landscape of the early twenty-first-century Philippines is no less active, and much more complicated. Working alongside continuously successful Tagalog pocketbooks are new platform companies, a growing competitor in English-language romance fiction, and an increasing number of transmedia stories and adaptations. The diversity of industry players in the Philippine romance industry is reflected in the texts themselves, as the different romance sectors have developed their own niche narrative conventions and genre histories. In the next chapter, we will zoom in closer on Tagalog pocketbook romance and #RomanceClass, in order to show the immensity and complexity of the Venn diagram that is Filipino romance publishing.

2 Filipino Romance Texts: From Tagalog Pocketbooks to #RomanceClass

How to Write a Tagalog Romance Novel begins with Apple Masallo likening romance to a queen (2011: 1). Katrina Stuart Santiago argues that the Filipino general public 'live off love and romance … culturally', supporting and sustaining this metaphor (2018: ix). Romantic movies frequently hit millions in box office sales. Love teams are regularly catapulted to stardom by being romantically involved in both fiction and real life. And then there is romance fiction, inarguably the 'queen' among genres in Filipino fiction, as 50 per cent of all fictional books released in the country each year belong to the category (Masallo, 2011: 3). This includes international imports but also a considerable amount of local media: for instance, Precious Hearts Romances – the 'biggest, most-loved, and most popular name in Tagalog romance' (Reyles, 2015: 8) – used to occupy the largest space in the Filipiniana section of National Bookstore, the country's most popular bookstore. Globally, romance fiction is often discussed in terms of inexhaustibility, and the reader in terms of voraciousness – as Diane Elam writes, '[t]here will always be room for another romance, since a reader can never read, a writer can never write, too many' (1992: 1). In the Philippines, we see an entire transmedia industry rooted in this promise, ensuring audience access to romance texts and media in many forms.

This chapter is on Filipino romance fiction – that is, the texts themselves. It is worth noting here that neither these texts nor their audiences are monolithic. Indeed, depending on several factors, including but certainly not limited to language and class, various texts and their audiences can be almost entirely discrete, circles in a Venn diagram with little overlap. Different sectors of the Filipino romance fiction market have specific demands and expectations of their romance texts as they address substantially different audiences. There is an intricate connection between the publishing enterprises in the Philippines and the markets they serve, explored in the previous chapter, and the texts that publishers produce. While the direct relationship between industry processes and textual output is theorised in the genre worlds framework, the extent to which these interlinked parts influence each other, and their relationships to language and class, is even more distinctive in the Philippines. One thing, however, remains reasonably common, a point of overlap in the Venn diagram: in engaging with romance fiction, Filipino audiences are seeking out the feeling of *kilig*.

Kilig is an affective state that encapsulates the overall 'feels' (Mithen, 2013) prompted by the experience of or involvement in anything romantic. This local term entered the *Oxford English Dictionary* in 2016, where its noun form is described as an 'exhilaration or elation caused by an exciting or romantic experience; an instance of this, a thrill' (Tan, 2016). It is 'a kind of affective romantic emotion – one that usually has a physical manifestation' (Parnell *et al.*, 2021a: 8; see also Trinidad, 2018; 2020). In the Philippines, romance is generally seen as synonymous with kilig because a key function of the genre is to engender kilig in the audience. 'Good' romance, therefore, might be measured by the levels of kilig it provokes (Santiago, 2018: 9).

It is worth noting here that, while romance is the queen of genres in the Philippines, kilig, and by extension romance, still receive a general level of cultural disapproval. Realism is the 'canonised' form of literature in the country (Reyes, 1991: 24), which comes with a concomitant assumption that the mandatory happy ending of romance fiction should be set aside to provide 'more real and grounded' stories about relationships by injecting 'stuff from real life', adding ambiguity and leaving complexities unresolved (Santiago, 2018: x). Occasionally, in an attempt to appeal to both romance lovers and those who hold that realism should be the dominant mode, texts might be tagged as 'not your ordinary romance' – but, upon closer inspection, they are not actually romances at all, as they do not end happily with the protagonists alive and together (de Guzman, Mori, Tan & Tanjutco, interview). Instead of kilig, these texts work to provoke *hugot*, which means to pull out something distressing in an attempt to stop the pain. Rather than the thrill and exhilaration of kilig, hugot is rooted in 'a bittersweet, love or pain resulting from a broken heart' (Luczon, 2019: 183).

This cultural disapprobation around romance fiction is not unique to the Philippines – indeed, the preface to American scholar Pamela Regis' seminal book on romance fiction is titled 'the most popular, least respected literary genre' (2003: xi). However, the notion that kilig should be subdued is one with more local specificity. 'Here in the Philippines it's hard to find a place where we're not judged', author Carla de Guzman told us (de Guzman, Mori, Tan & Tanjutco, interview).

For her, #RomanceClass became that place: 'this is that place for me where I feel safe to feel things, to talk about things . . . it's okay to find these things kilig' (de Guzman, Mori, Tan & Tanjutco, interview).

All this said, the production of kilig-worthy romance narratives with happy endings continues apace in the Philippines. Its appeal is 'eternal' (Lifestyle Inquirer, 2016), providing the 'most exciting escape' fantasies in line with the needs and wants of its readers (Santiago, 2018: xi). The continued popularity of romance sits against a harsh social, economic, and political backdrop. The pressure from the reading public, craving kilig and a happy ending, is far greater than any pressure to reimagine the genre in a more realist mode and thus the reign of Queen Romance continues.

However, as noted above, there are distinct domains in her queendom. Texts and readerships are not at all homogeneous. There is a clear demarcation by preferred language, which means that the crossover between readerships is slim. In this chapter, we discuss the narrative conventions of two distinct kinds of Filipino romance fiction: Tagalog pocketbook romance (whose use of language serves as a pattern for many works posted on Wattpad) and English-language romance published by #RomanceClass. These are by no means the only two types of romance fiction in the Philippines, but, because they have such different readerships and textual conventions, they are a useful pair of illustrative examples around how texts respond differently to the specific needs and desires of their audiences.

2.1 Tagalog Pocketbook Romance: Language, Audience, and Textual Conventions

Usually composed of ten chapters that span up to 90–100 pages, Tagalog pocketbook romances are 'paperbacks with glossy covers and newsprint leaves' (Jurilla, 2008: 264). The materials used in the production of the novels are low cost, and they are consequently sold cheaply. This makes them triply accessible: they are short, handy, and inexpensive.

Tagalog romance pocketbooks are written in Taglish – a hybrid of Tagalog (the vernacular language of Manila and surrounding regions) and English (the language of power and domination, established by American imperialism) – and as such can be easily understood by the majority of the

Filipino reading public, including those from Classes D–E. Language in the Philippines is intrinsically tied to questions of influence, power, and class. The ability to speak and write in English comes with connotations of superiority because command of the language generally comes from the kind of education exclusive to Classes A–C. Speakers of local languages who do not have full command of English are often belittled, with condescending terms for them entering the popular vocabulary: for example, 'Carabao English', a term first used by comics creator Tony Velasquez to refer to the language used by an 'illiterate Filipino who spoke and was not understood by the English-speaking elite because his words straddled two linguistic worlds of Tagalog and English' (Reyes, 2009: 8). If the use of 'Carabao English' represents an attempt from Filipinos in lower social classes to adapt to the language of colonial masters, another term, *bakya*, refers to favouring only the local and vernacular. This term is commonly and derisively used to describe the masses who prefer watching Tagalog movies over Hollywood ones, categorising their tastes as 'cheap, gauche, naïve, and provincial', highlighting the lasting impacts of American colonialism in the Philippines (Lacaba, 1983: 117).

Taglish, however – the language of romance pocketbooks, as well Filipino Wattpad stories (especially ones that are traditionally published by Bliss Books) – has the capacity to mediate the separate experiences and sensibilities caused by speaking exclusively in either English or Tagalog. It avoids not just the elitist stigma of English as a 'superior' language but also the old-fashioned use of Tagalog, which does not bear a strong resemblance to the contemporary ways in which the language is spoken. Taglish has ended up as a lingua franca that serves as a meeting point for Filipinos coming from different social classes. The use of Taglish in romance pocketbooks has been described as the genre's 'biggest innovation' (Reyles, 2015: 11), as it allows readers who find works written in either a more refined English or Tagalog – the most common languages of publication – inaccessible. They not only offer stories that are easy to read and understand for a wider Filipino audience but also promote a dignified view of characters who are adept in both languages (Reyles, 2015: 11).

Tagalog pocketbook romance is centred primarily on poverty, as this is the experience of a substantial part of its audience. These texts tend to depict characters that reflect the 'vast gap in economics and sensibilities between social classes in the Philippines' (Jurilla, 2008: 280). They are produced primarily for a female audience, mainly from Classes D–E, described by Reyes as 'market vendors, office employees, students, housemaids, and housewives' (2001: 38). The nature of the audience shapes the conventions and pleasures of the books, responding to their specific needs and desires. According to Deinla and Dressel, a 2016 survey by the National Economic and Development Authority (NEDA) suggested that the typical Filipino had 'middle class [Class C] aspirations' – that is, to live an economically and socially comfortable life 'living in a medium-sized home, owning a car, having enough money to cover their daily needs, and affording good education for their children' (Deinla & Dressel, 2019: 18). As Class D and E citizens earn an average annual income of around PHP 191, 000 (US$3,968) and PHP 62,000 (US$1,288) respectively (the average annual income for Class C is around PHP 629,000 or US$11,000), Tagalog pocketbook romance is a key site in which middle-class aspirations can be explored. Therefore, the central fantasy developed is usually to escape poverty – they allow the reader to 'leave the familiar world [of poverty] behind, but only for the moment' (Reyes, 1991: 28). In the real world, problems associated with poverty are intricate, complex, and structural, but pocketbook romances offer readers a linear, direct, and clear fictive resolution to these problems. Their conventions and formulae make social mobility possible through romance, resolving the convoluted crises and never-ending uncertainties experienced in real-world poverty (Reyes, 1991: 27).

2.1.1 Convention 1: Rich and Cosmopolitan Hero

At the heart of nearly every Tagalog pocketbook romance is a rich boy/poor girl pairing. This dynamic is so ubiquitous as to become a stereotype of these novels (Barrios, 2001: 293; Reyes, 2001: 44). In her guide to writing pocketbook romance, Masallo explicitly characterised the hero as 'richer than the heroine' (2011: 24). The pairing of a 'rich, handsome, smart young man' and a 'modest and simple woman from the lower middle class' has been in a classic theme in Filipino fiction for a long time (Reyes, 1982: 77), a successful fictional formula where romantic love provides a simple solution to the reality of class divide (Santiago, 2018: 29). In this sense, pocketbook romances present a utopian outlook, erasing class differences that are extremely difficult to navigate in real life through associating the abstract promise of everlasting love with the concrete evidence of a comfortable life that is to be accessed by the heroine at the end of the narrative.

The rich, cosmopolitan hero is the central textual representation of this promise. He often has parents who are protective of their social class (which can be the story's major conflict) and frequently uses English in his dialogue, positioning him as educated, modern, and urban. He is also – at least initially – unapproachable. As Joi Barrios notes, 'mysterious', 'aloof', and 'grouchy' are listed as some of a hero's most important characteristics before their romantic relationship with the heroine blossoms (2001: 292). This unapproachability is associated with the hero's wealth, fame, and influence, rooted in an inborn entitlement not to be friendly with people they perceive to be ordinary or of a lower social standing, including the heroine – but, of course, this changes over the course of the novel as they fall in love.

We can see a typical example of this kind of hero in Keene Alicante's *Then and Now*, where hero Ace is introduced in the following manner:

> Augustus Caesar Gela IV, the infamous 'Ace' of their school, was one of their school's outstanding students. He was the Student Council president, he was the CAT corps commander, and he was the captain of their basketball varsity team. Halos kalahati rin ng populasyon ng mga kababaihan sa kanilang eskuwelahan ay crush ito [Almost half of the school's female population also has a crush on him] because aside from the fact that he was an achiever, it was also matched by his undeniably boyish looks. (2007: 1)

The novel's first chapter is a flashback to the high school life of the protagonists, where heroine Maja pined over the coveted hero Ace. However, Ace completely disregarded Maja, leaving her heartbroken. As a result, she channelled her energy into developing her career, which leads to her being reunited with Ace: she is the executive secretary in the Bona Dea group of companies, and he is revealed to be heir apparent to the company's CEO. His social status and continued upward mobility are reinforced over and over again: he is a 'managing director of a foreign capital consulting group based in the US . . . that was near bankruptcy but was saved by his brilliant mind' on top of 'graduating from Yale with highest honors and had two masterals [Masters degrees] at a very young age', and he has 'also been running two different businesses in the US aside from the fact that he still had the capital consulting group in his hand' (Alicante, 2007: 114). This elicits a crisis of self-confidence in Maja as she begins to see herself (again) as unworthy of the attention of a man like Ace when confronted with his accomplishments, which is compounded by her internalised classism.

Listing hero characters' accomplishments is only one of the ways in which their social position and success are made clear in pocketbook romances. Affluence is also typified through glamorous settings and luxurious displays of wealth, such as mansions, rest houses, and cars, which should either be 'Mercedes or BMW and not Kia Pride' (Barrios, 2001: 292). One particular example of this is the presence of swimming pools, which, alongside things like jacuzzis and bath-tubs, demonstrate a hero's unlimited access to water – something completely inaccessible to the majority of Filipino people living in poverty (Barrios, 2001: 280). Interestingly, scenes involving swimming pools are often key in the hero's journey towards recognising the hidden beauty of the heroine, even though she is from a lower class than himself (Barrios, 2001: 281), as can be seen in the following scene in *Undercover Maid*:

> Nahulog siya sa swimming pool . . . Nakatitig ito sa dibdib niyang bakat na bakat sa suot niyang uniporme dahil basa . . . Bumaba pa ang mga mata nito at sinuyod ng tingin ang basang kabuuan niya. [She fell in the swimming pool . . . He was lusting after her breasts that were revealed by her wet uniform . . . His eyes even traveled throughout her whole being.] He smiled crookedly when he finally met her eyes. "Very nice . . . " he teased . . . How could a maid look as delectable as that? He smiled naughtily. She was not his type. But she is really pretty and she has a nice butt. (Lee, 2006: 34–7)

Her very literal immersion in his world, it seems, allows him to begin to come to terms with his desire for her – first, here, his sexual desire and then eventually, as he comes to know her better, his desire to be with her romantically – and his unapproachable façade begins to melt away.

More prosaically, though, displays of wealth like the swimming pool serve as proof of the ability of the hero to financially provide for the heroine. This is often presented literally in plots where the hero employs the heroine in some capacity, providing for her in a professional capacity long before their romantic involvement begins. This kind of situation permits forced proximity between the protagonists, who otherwise might not encounter each other owing to their respective social classes. Their unequal status forces the heroine to learn to adjust to the rules, needs, and wants of her male employer to avoid risking her livelihood and simultaneously to express her indebtedness for being allowed access to such a luxurious, affluent space (Barrios, 2001: 280). This is epitomised in a scene from the novel *Business and Pleasure*:

> 'I need a PA. Be ready tomorrow, six a.m. sharp,' malamig niyang sabi saka kinagatan ang malamig na pizza [he coldly told her while munching a cold slice of pizza].

> 'Eh?' dumbfounded nitong tanong [she dumbfoundedly asked].

> 'I need a PA so be ready tomorrow six a.m sharp,' ulit niya sa parehong tono habang patuloy sa pagkain [he repeated in the same tone while continuing to eat].

> . . .

> 'Pero ayoko.' Napatuwid ito ng tayo. ['But I don't want to.' She straightened her posture].

> . . .

'Saan ka nga ulit nakatira?' malamig niyang untag.
Nakaramdam siya ng sadistic pleasure nang makita ang panla-
laki ng mga mata nito sa pagkagulat. ['Where do you live
again?' he coldly reiterated. He then felt sadistic pleasure when
he saw how her eyes enlarged in shock.] (Masallo, 2011: 22–3)

In this charged space, where all the power dynamics unquestionably favour
the hero, sexist language is frequently used. Barrios notes that English in
particular is used by the hero to put the heroine 'in her place', evident in
phrases such as 'silly woman' and 'real doll' (2001: 282). It is in the figure of
the hero that the intersection between gender, class, and language dominance converge. Just as the English term 'real doll' positions women as
beautiful objects to be owned, in Tagalog it implies ownership of the
heroine. This idea is reflected in many titles of Tagalog pocketbooks;
Reyes points to examples such as *Oo, Ako'y Iyo* (Yes, I am yours), *Akin
ka . . . Sa Buong Buhay Mo* (You are mine . . . all throughout your life), and
Lahat ng Araw, Lahat ng Gabi . . . Sa Akin (All the days, all the nights . . .
are mine) (2001: 36).

While the dynamic of rich hero/poor heroine is pervasive in Filipino
romance fiction, the inverse (rich heroine/poor hero) is also an accepted
trope in Tagalog pocketbooks (Barrios, 2001: 293). This alternative char-
acterisation positions the heroine as an aspirational figure for romance's
predominantly female readership because of the character's financial stabi-
lity. This popular trope is embedded within the marketing of Tagalog
pocketbooks; Precious Hearts Romances, for instance, has a romance line
titled *Señorito* and *Señorita*, which features romances by Rose Tan, a brand
name author in the Philippines. These Spanish terms are used locally by
Filipino servants to politely address their employers, thus highlighting the
financial dynamic between the romantic protagonists in these novels, and
further reinforcing the classist dimensions inherent in the trope.

2.1.2 Convention 2: Fierce Heroines

Despite all of the ways in which heroes are imbued with power, Tagalog
pocketbook romances do not necessarily render women powerless.
Although they might be forced into obedience by their class position, the

novels often also highlight their 'liberated and modern' status as an aspirational representation for many readers (Lucero, 1991: 146). As an archetype, the liberated fierce woman is usually marked by her ability to confront the hero with snarky remarks, no matter how enormous the gap between their social standings. Much of her critique of the hero comes through her inner monologue, but this is interspersed with outbursts in pure Tagalog: something which not only adds to dramatic effect (Barrios, 2001: 283) but also offers catharsis for the readers who speak the same language but do not have the opportunity to shout back at their own employers without endangering their livelihood (Jurilla, 2008: 289).

These heroines are often reticent about romantic love and attempt to govern their hearts so they do not fall in love (usually with the hero). To return to *Then and Now* (Alicante, 2007), heroine Maja repeatedly reminds herself that she will not be foolish enough to fall in love with the wealthy man who broke her heart in high school. Similarly, Lailani, the heroine of *Undercover Maid* (Lee, 2006), goes to work as a maid for famous athlete Jett as part of a plan to avenge her sister, based on the belief that he has victimised her (which ultimately turns out to be false): she is determined to hate him, not love him. These heroines are not shy and retiring but bold and determined. More specifically, these fierce heroines are determined to exercise rigid control over their emotions in the presence of wealthy men who they know will hurt them. However, as seen in the following excerpt from *Then and Now*, this is challenged when they encounter the hero's more admirable side, which might then prompt lengthy self-loathing for their inability to stop themselves falling in love:

> Since the day she admitted to herself she still had feelings for him, she couldn't look at him in the eye already. And she wanted to hate herself for that. Because no matter how she told herself Ace wasn't the guy worthy of her love, she just couldn't stop that.
>
> She wanted to blame something or someone why she was feeling that way towards him but she couldn't find ond. At sino naman kaya ang sisisihin niya? Ang puso niya dahil sa dinami-rami naman ng lalaki ay kay Augustus Caesar pa

> iyon natutong magmahal? ... Pesteng puso talaga! [And
> who would she blame? Her heart just because it had decided
> to fall for Augustus Caesar instead of any other men? Oh
> heart! What a pest.] (Alicante, 2007: 90)

The phrase 'Ace wasn't the guy worthy of her love' is particularly
notable here. Given the skewed power dynamics, the heroines are not
wrong to be distrustful of these powerful men: their fierceness is
warranted. However, the hero's acceptance of the heroine's fierce
attitude – in *Then and Now*, this is signalled by Ace simply not firing
Maja when she yells at him in Tagalog – textually represents his
worthiness of her love, as someone who will take care of her, treat her
lovingly, and accept her fierceness.

2.1.3 Convention 3: 'Love' Scenes, Not 'Sex' Scenes

The heroine spends a considerable amount of time restraining herself in
Tagalog pocketbook romances: from voicing her thoughts, prohibiting
herself from showing weakness by falling in love, to forbidding herself to
fall apart when she and the hero inevitably go through a period of separation
before the achieving their happy ending (especially when she sees herself as
someone undeserving of his love). The representations of characters and
events in Tagalog romances are influenced by editorial guidelines imposed
by publishers. These directions extend to displays of intimacy between
characters and representations of sex. Responding to market expectations,
Books for Pleasure, for instance, stipulated in their publishing guidelines
that there should be no explicit sex, but the novel should not be too
'Victorian' (Jurilla, 2008: 179). Precious Pages, while less conservative in
their approach, specified that authors describe lovemaking in a 'romantic
way' (Jurilla, 2008: 179). This convention of romantic sex in Tagalog
romances has been further codified in Masallo's *How to Write a Tagalog
Romance*, where she describes intimate scenes as 'love scenes' rather than
'sex scenes' as they should contain more romance than graphic sexual details
(2011: 50). This approach to sex in Filipino romance is largely market
driven and underpinned by the cultural dynamics of the Philippines, where,
broadly speaking, Tagalog pocketbook romance fiction aligns itself with

local Catholic understandings of love and intimacy; specifically, the principle that 'nothing was to be done in excess' (Reyes, 2012: 34).

On top of regulating the depiction of sex on the page, there are strong conventions in place about the language used in such scenes. Love scenes are almost always written in English, exemplifying a belief that it is vulgar and taboo to use the local vernacular in naming body parts and describing sex. Masallo advises that Tagalog should only be used in these scenes when an intensification of emotion needs to be delivered, noting that only English is considered to be sophisticated enough to convey any mechanics of sex in the narrative without being crude (2011).

As noted, conventions around love scenes are largely dictated by editors and publishers. Segundo Matias of Precious Pages Corporation has stated that a heroine must always be a virgin, which is an archetypal depiction of a morally good woman in Filipino literary and popular culture (Reyles, 2015: 11). Patterned after the Virgin Mary, the virgin heroine's value of restraint can be compared to Mary Magdalene, 'who is seen as a transgressor and figure of excess' (Reyes, 2012: 29). It is also worth noting that the third most popular type of romance in the country is 'inspirational' romance, which 'contains explicit Christian themes' (Masallo, 2011: 13) and is further reflective of the strong Catholic influence on pocketbook romance publishing.

However, in response to the success of Filipino stories on Wattpad – which share a considerable amount of DNA with pocketbook romance, especially as regards their use of language – some traditional publishers have carved out new digital spaces where these rules are relaxed somewhat and authors are permitted to write things which would not be acceptable in tradition print publications such as Precious Hearts Romances. One such author is Mandie Lee, who, through Booklat (a digital arm of Precious Pages Corporation), published *My Genie Lover* (2014), a light fantasy softcore erotic romance tagged by readers as 'sexy rom-com' (Heruela *et al.*, 2015: 140). Moving away from the traditional world of print publishing meant that Lee had more authorial freedom, in that her story would not be censored and her sex scenes cut short (Heruela *et al.*, 2015: 140). Whether or not this signals the beginning of a broader shift in pocketbook romance remains to be seen; however, it is indicative of the effect that Wattpad stories have had on this section of the Filipino romance market. This autonomy from established textual conventions has been fully embraced by authors in #RomanceClass who, through their self-publishing praxis, actively respond to and introduce new alternatives to traditional Filipino romance fiction.

2.2 The Alternative Conventions of #RomanceClass Texts

The #RomanceClass community produces very different texts from the Tagalog pocketbook romances. This is true not only in terms of language – #RomanceClass books are all in English – but also in terms of the kinds of stories they tell. They have moved significantly away from the Madonna (moral)/Magdalena (immoral) dichotomy and have reworked numerous romance conventions in order to access an almost entirely different audience, offering Filipino romance with a different flavour.

Mina V. Esguerra, the founder of #RomanceClass, notes that the decision to write in English stems from her confidence in using the language: it is her first language and the one she knows how to 'speak well and write well' (RomanceClass, 2020). However, she is well aware that Tagalog pocketbook romance is immensely popular, even though its use of vernacular language means that it gets significantly less respect than fiction written in English. This obvious difference in language usage exemplifies the fact that Filipino romance has 'totally different sets of readers sometimes' (RomanceClass, 2020). In the Philippines, the audience for #RomanceClass are those who have the capacity to read English easily and for leisure, which, as noted above, denotes a certain level of education which is typically congruent with social class. This means that the texts have quite different priorities and pleasures, and are far less focused on the fantasy of escape from poverty into a better (or even luxurious) life through the romantic happy ending. Instead, we might argue, the central fantasies here are about inclusion, equality, and social progressiveness.

2.2.1 Alternative 1: Reshaping Female and Queer Characters

Because they are not necessarily centred on heroines whose lives need to be materially more comfortable by the end of the story, #Romance Class is able to portray heroines with a variety of different careers.

While #RomanceClass heroines do sometimes grapple with the realities of poverty and precarious labour – see, for instance, Jo (a sex worker) and Liza (a department store worker), the two heroines of Brigitte Bautista's *You, Me, U.S.* (2019) – there is a far higher proportion of heroines with secure, financially comfortable professions, such as wedding planner Daphne in *Better at Weddings Than You* (Esguerra, 2017a), tour guide Naya in *What Kind of Day* (Esguerra, 2018), restoration architect Giada in *Dare to Love* (Santi, 2016), and the women in STEM who populate the works of Celestine Trinidad and Six de los Reyes. This means that heroines are not obliged to be submissive or obedient to heroes, as they often are in pocketbook romance, because they are usually not financially dependent on them.

The alternative possibilities for heroines present in #RomanceClass books sometimes shock audiences. When we interviewed her, Esguerra fondly narrated an experience when #RomanceClass held a live reading at a Philippines science high school where many of the students were surprised that characters in the books belonged to professions they did not know existed, for instance. Esguerra used this opportunity to convince the audience that these stories can not only show viable career options for students but also validate the idea that Filipinos can be good at these jobs (Radyo Katipunan 87.9, 2021). From then on, #RomanceClass, via Esguerra's directives, encouraged writers 'to write about their careers or careers they are familiar with', especially if these are not represented prominently in the media they consume (Radyo Katipunan 87.9, 2021). To illustrate this, Esguerra talked about C. P. Santi, whose background as an architect inspired her to portray characters like Martin in 'Only the Beginning' from *Promdi Heart (Hometown Love Stories)* (2017), a heritage architect from Manila, involved in visiting, surveying, and conserving heritage sites in Jimenez, Misamis Occidental. The central fantasy is not experiencing abrupt social mobility, as it is in pocketbook romance, but designing aspirational careers for characters with ideal setups and models. For instance, Santi was able to portray a speculative professional world for her conservation architect character 'where everything works', from financial aid getting effectively distributed to the agencies involved showing the utmost support for the conservation project (RomanceClass, 2021).

Similarly, sometimes #RomanceClass books invert the popular rich male boss/poor female subordinate paradigm of pocketbook romance. For instance, Carla de Guzman's *How She Likes It* (2018) is the story of a relationship between a female make-up company CEO and her male secretary (who is also a single parent), which sharply critiques the limitations the patriarchal status quo places on both men and women. The following rant from the heroine neatly summarises the book's critique:

> 'God.' Isabel sighed, rubbing her hands over her face. Was it so hard to believe that someone could have it all? Couldn't a woman run a business, have babies, help other people? 'We really have to change the board. That's such an old-fashioned way of thinking'. (de Guzman, 2018: 141)

Not subscribing to the much resented 'old-fashioned way of thinking' (de Guzman, 2018: 141), the narrative also flips the recommended ages for protagonists in pocketbook romance: according to Masallo, the pocketbook romance hero, in his late twenties to early thirties, is supposed to be 'older than the heroine', who is between twenty-three and twenty-eight, presenting another way in which the unequal power dynamic between the two characters is reinforced (2011: 23–8). In *How She Likes It*, however, the heroine is older and established while the hero is a younger man still finding his footing in life. This dynamic is also present in Agay Llanera's *Mango Summer* (2018). Heroine Fiona is thirty-six, the owner and manager of a mango farm. Hero Greg – pointedly nicknamed 'G-Boy' – is twenty-eight and is a visitor in Fiona's sphere of influence. Due to a harvest of sour mangoes, the farm is in trouble, but Greg does not save Fiona or dictate her choices: rather, he supports her and her decisions and helps her when she needs and/or asks for it. Both *How She Likes It* and *Mango Summer* are clear examples of the support shown by #RomanceClass for character dynamics significantly different from those dictated in Tagalog pocketbook romance publishing.

#RomanceClass unabashedly centres the local Filipino reader. However, because their books are in English and are published on global digital platforms like Amazon, they also offer an international audience alternative representations of Filipino people. Foreign media and publications regularly rely on stereotypes and assumptions when portraying Filipinos – usually as migrant workers who are tasked to serve foreign employers (Radyo Katipunan 87.9, 2021). #RomanceClass, however, presents a distinctly different image of Filipino people, which allows them not just to show their local readership a range of career prospects but also to show international readers that 'these jobs exist, we [Filipinos] can be the boss, and that we can be good at it' (Radyo Katipunan 87.9, 2021).

#RomanceClass's project around representation is by no means limited to professions – they have a strong emphasis on highlighting minority and under-represented identities. For instance, Carla de Guzman's *If the Dress Fits* (2017) pushes back against hegemonic ideas of female beauty. Barrios notes that making heroines fat is inapt (2001: 290) but in this book, de Guzman explicitly centres a fat heroine. The community also demonstrates a commitment to tackle under-discussed contemporary issues, such as mental health, which is central to Celestine Trinidad's *Ghost of a Feeling* (2018). If at the heart of Tagalog pocketbook romance are class aspirations and class struggles, with concomitant fantasies arising from those, #RomanceClass, in addressing an English-speaking audience who presumably have a much more privileged class position, has room to dwell on more varied cultural categories than class, and map the complexities of gender, sexuality, race, and ethnicity as well.

One clear example of this is in #RomanceClass's commitment to producing queer romance novels. These do not exist in pocketbook romance, which is described as a 'conservative genre' (Reyes, 2001: 42) and which 'ideally, only includes a heterosexual pairing' (Masallo, 2011: 12). In #RomanceClass, however, queer romance is not only welcome but encouraged, especially from writers who are queer themselves. We interviewed several such authors, including Chi Yu Rodriguez and Brigitte Bautista, who wrote the community's first bisexual character and F/F romance respectively. Both mentioned how their writing of these romances was driven by their own experiences in high school. As they spent formative years in Catholic schools, both describe how these institutions became witness to 'the whole fumbling with sexuality in an all-girls school' (Rodriguez, interview) and how 'ridiculous the rules of engagement in these spaces are' (Bautista, interview). While these subjects are not covered in pocketbook romance, they are not absent from Philippine literature more broadly: as another of our interviewees, Ronald Lim, noted, 'the Philippines has a really rich LGBTQ literature history' (interview). However, these texts are rarely genre romance – as Lim went on to say:

> it's either erotica or literature with a capital L. And usually in these works it's either somebody's pining for someone, the gay guy dies with just like, yeah … Or it's erotica, it's sex, which is great, but you know sometimes you want a happy ending. (Interview)

Bautista's first book, *Don't Tell My Mother*, was traditionally published by Anvil, but the notes they provided on her second manuscript, which would become *You, Me, U.S.*, reflect this: they wanted a much stronger focus on 'discovering one's self and identity' than she was interested in writing (Bautista, interview). Self-publishing with #RomanceClass opened up different possibilities – not least, it regularly affords queer characters their 'plain old good happy ending' (Lim, interview). This, as seen very clearly in *Start Here* (Lim & Bautista, 2018), a dedicated queer romance anthology revolving around first encounters, goes strongly against the grain of the types of queer representation usually seen in Philippine fiction and media.

2.2.2 Alternative 2: Decentring Manila

Romance fiction in the Philippines has historically been influenced by not just hegemonic ideologies around gender and sexuality but also the consistent centring of Manila. When the #RomanceClass community was in its early stages, many authors instinctively wrote about characters from Manila 'because that's all they ever read, because that was all that was ever published' (Radyo Katipunan 87.9, 2021). While many #RomanceClass novels still take place in the nation's capital, clear community directives that Manila need not be the setting and the space it provides to reconsider genre norms mean there are also now many which push beyond, situating romance in other parts of the Philippines, rural and urban. This was abetted by the online set-up of the class via Facebook and email, which meant that a lot of aspiring authors who were not in and/or from Manila could join (Esguerra, interview). The use of English also assisted here – in many areas outside Manila, vernacular languages other than Tagalog are spoken, making English a sort of universal leveller: something Esguerra identified after exploring the possibility of translating her work into other Filipino languages (Radyo Katipunan 87.9, 2021).

#RomanceClass authors who predominantly set their works outside Manila include Clarisse David, who lives and sets her romances in Iloilo; C. P. Santi, who writes predominantly about municipalities in the provinces of Misamis Occidental and Laguna, where there are sites she usually visits as a conservation architect; and Chris Mariano, who writes about Aklan, where she grew up (RomanceClass, 2021). In the #RomanceClass podcast episode entitled 'The Philippines As Our Setting', Santi and Mariano agreed that setting in narrative 'is more than just a place' (RomanceClass, 2021). In the same way that community beta readers and editors ensure that Manila is represented accurately – through, for example, ensuring that traffic is represented like real Manila traffic (de Guzman, Mori, Tan & Tanjutco, interview) – Santi and Mariano argue that the location in their works should textualise the rich history of the place and the lived experiences of its citizens (RomanceClass, 2021). In *Cover Story Girl* (2014), for instance, Mariano represents Boracay in Aklan not just as a tourist destination with famous white beaches and bustling nightlife but as a place with rich history through the use of a character who works at the local heritage museum. Similarly, in 'Drummer Boy' (2017), Mariano represents Aklan's Ati-Atihan festival, a week of collective merrymaking, which unveils some of the area's hidden gems and specific locations (RomanceClass, 2021). Locating a story outside Manila means not just rendering the setting but also the characters, who need to feel local. This is something Santi tries to achieve through the use of vernacular phrases and idioms, noting that talking to people, appreciating the jokes they find funny, and knowing their day-to-day activities and beliefs infuses the work with a hyperlocal flavour (RomanceClass, 2021). Interestingly, this often results in her protagonists building close relationships with parish priests. When asked about this in an interview, Santi explained that it arises from her own experiences of being part of the communities she encounters in her work as a cultural heritage conservation worker who regularly visits and surveys Spanish colonial churches (Peralta, 2017).

Representing a variety of places and characters also allows #RomanceClass's global readers to experience the Philippines in a way that does not solely focus on city living in Metro Manila. Pushing back against assumptions which locate Manila as the exclusive locus of the 'contemporary' and the 'modern' in the Philippines, this provides a more complex understanding of the Filipino experience (something which is heavily problematised in academia, especially in history and literary studies, as they wrestle with the entangled concepts of national identity and nation building). This opens up further opportunities for RomanceClass authors: it is worth noting that RomanceClass author Carla de Guzman has published two books traditionally through Carina (an imprint of the North America-based romance publishing powerhouse Harlequin), which are both set in Lipa, not Manila.

2.2.3 Alternative 3: Sex and Heat Levels

As discussed above, pocketbook romance takes quite a conservative line in its depiction of sex (even if the rise of Wattpad books is leading to more experimentation in digital spaces). #RomanceClass, however, takes a different approach. Their books can be sorted and filtered on their website via 'heat levels'. Readers who do not wish to read on-the-page sex can find books that will meet their needs, but readers looking for more explicit content can also find it. The heat level is a scale that is something of a contract between authors and readers, and works as follows:

0. No sex on or off page
1. Off-page sex mentioned in story
2. At least one 'closed door' sex scene
3. At least one 'open door' sex scene
4. Explicit erotic romance with HEA/HFN. (Esguerra, 2020a)

The heat levels are a manifestation of the community's dedication to sex positivity. As one author puts it, in #RomanceClass, 'there is no shame in sex, in engaging in sex and wanting to have sex' (de Guzman, Mori, Tan &

Tanjutco, interview), which is very different from the conventions around sex in Tagalog pocketbook romance. Treating sex as a spectrum rather than an either/or allows readers to read to their comfort level. The community's sex-positive agenda does not sidestep the reality that there are some members who uphold Catholic tradition and would prefer not to write or read work with higher heat levels (Lim, interview).

The community's practices around writing sex scenes have evolved organically but deliberately. Esguerra notes that in the very first class she ran in 2013, none of the students wrote sex scenes, although their work featured characters 'in their 20s and even 30s' (interview). She chalks this up to the local romantic media they had been consuming (like pocketbook romances), in which sex was not part of the narrative. In order to push back against this, she urged everyone in the next class to try writing sex scenes, advising anyone who was not comfortable doing so to just wait for the next class to join (Esguerra, interview) – an example of the community's ethos of care, which will be discussed in more depth in Chapter 3. This ethos of care around sex scenes is not centred solely on authors but extends to readers. The community guidelines state that all sex must be 'consensual, responsible, and hot (ie not bad sex, not punishment)' (RomanceClass, n.d.a). There are no formal avenues for sex education in the country, even though HIV cases are on the rise among young people. #RomanceClass expresses care towards its readers through emphasising the importance of contraception and normalising (and eroticising) consent. See, for example, this sex scene from de Guzman's *How She Likes It*:

> 'We have to move, I'm too tall–'
>
> 'No,' she insisted, shaking her head as she reached for his cock, raking her nails lightly over it. *'I like it this way. Glove on, please.'*
>
> 'Yes boss,' he said, and he tried to ignore the red flush of embarrassment that marred his cheeks all the way down to his chest, *making Isabel laugh as he put on protection.* Her body was flush against his, his arms supporting his weight as he slowly slid his covered cock between her legs. *Safety first, obviously.* (2019: 154, our emphasis)

If we read this alongside an intimate scene from a pocketbook romance – Lee's *Undercover Maid* (2006), for instance – we can see marked differences. Contraception, for example, might not simply be forgotten but actually deliberately set aside as a textual example of a hero's readiness to commit to a possibly impregnated heroine:

> 'Bakit hindi ka ... bakit hindi ka gumamit ng ...' ['Why did you not ... why did you not use ...']
>
> 'Ng?' [Use what?]
>
> 'Ng ... proteksyon?' Hindi niya napigil ang pamumula ng mukha ['Use ... protection?' She couldn't stop herself from blushing.]
>
> Sa inis niya tumaas pa ang isang sulok ng mga labi nito. [In annoyance, he raised the corner of his lips.] 'Because ... I wanted to feel you.'
>
> She blushed even more at the thought of what he said. 'Paano kung ... mabuntis ako?' [What if I get pregnant?]
>
> Lumuwang pa ang ngiti nito. [He smiled brightly.] 'So what?' (Lee, 2006: 81)

> ' ... I just wanted to prove that when it comes to you, it's not just sex. We're making love. And the first time I ever made love was with you. You should know why ... I was ready for the consequences. I knew it would be okay if I got you pregnant. I was ready to take the responsibility'. (Lee, 2006: 94)

The community's commitment to positive and responsible representation of sex took work – they have, for instance, run workshops where 'difficult conversations' around what consent is and what it looks like took place (Esguerra, interview). The 'consensual, responsible and hot' provision is now in their textbook, making it a core tenet of #RomanceClass. As one author told us, books that do not adhere to the principle are books 'we do not want to read' (de Guzman, Mori, Tan & Tanjutco, interview).

2.3 Romance Market versus Romance Community

Tagalog pocketbook romance and the English-language romance novels produced by #RomanceClass are not the only kinds of romance fiction or media in the Philippines; however, reading them alongside each other is illustrative of how siloed the local romance market is. Pocketbook romances, which are written in the vernacular Taglish and are dominated by fantasies of upward mobility, target the social classes who do not necessarily have mastery over the colonial language English. #RomanceClass books, however, are in English, which pitches them to a Class A–C audience (which, along with the fact they are published digitally globally alongside local print editions, also makes them accessible to the broader international Anglophone market). They are – broadly – not so concerned with the economic issues of poverty that a large section of the Filipino population wrestles with, dealing instead with representations of gender, sexuality, ethnicity, and race. We can see here not just two distinct markets but two distinct approaches to the complexity of 'Filipino-ness'. While pocketbook romance centres what could be considered the main concern of a postcolony that now belongs to the global South, #RomanceClass embraces the possibilities of a messier depiction of the 'Filipino', who is already an amalgamation of cultural markers and identities.

This chapter has focused primarily on the texts themselves, but there is one more consideration which should enter into any analysis of these two forms of romance. Tagalog pocketbook romance (and its descendant, Wattpad romance) is a highly profitable sector of the publishing industry. In 2001, when books were priced up to PHP 30 (US$0.52), publishers would release 4–12 titles per month that sold around 5,000 to 20,000 copies each (Barrios, 2001). This mode of operation allowed them to promise authors a full-time career that is 'far from the image of the struggling writer' (Reyles, 2015: 13) and publishers significant lucrative income (Jurilla, 2008). This can extensively finance growth-oriented projects, such as the establishment of Precious's very own Precious Pages Building in 2015, which not only serves as the company's headquarters, administrative office, and event centre but is 'physical and monumental proof of its success and legacy' (Reyles, 2015: 13).

The same is not necessarily true, however, of #RomanceClass: '[w]e're not getting rich', one author told us (de Guzman, Mori, Tan & Tanjutco, interview). This fact feeds into the textual priorities and conventions discussed above. The politics of the Tagalog pocketbook romance might not exactly be progressive; however, their fantasy of social mobility through romantic love is very popular. This offers clear capitalist incentives for this sector of the romance publishing market to continue producing this kind of material. Traditional publishers' capital *is* tradition: by continuously reproducing this long-held convention of class mobility through romance, the books are 'sold to us like a product that we need – a necessity, a requirement' (Santiago, 2018: 4). However, as Santiago notes, we should be very wary of simply positioning the reader of pocketbook romance as a dupe (2018: 3). It is clear through self-aware lines and dialogue that critique some of the genre's established conventions that these books sometimes wink at themselves. They are inside jokes, and the readership is in on them.

#RomanceClass has strikingly different priorities from the traditionally very profit-driven Tagalog pocketbook romance industry. They think of themselves and their readers as being in a community, rather than a more neoliberal creator–consumer relationship, which manifests in an ethos of care. Because of this, they are less interested in figuring out what makes money and then producing more of the same, and more in exploring alternatives to existing romance publishing conventions, pushing for more inclusion and representation, and espousing a socially progressive agenda. Essentially, we might argue, they privilege empowerment of the community over financial enrichment. The community model they have developed offers solutions to some of the problems of the Filipino romance publishing industry (industrial and textual) and alternatives to others. It is to a deeper exploration of this fascinating collective that we turn in the next chapter.

3 Collectivity and Care: The Case of #RomanceClass Sociality

The previous two chapters in this book have explored what a Filipino romance novel is and the landscape for publishing them in the twenty-first century. As we have shown, the answers to these questions are neither simple nor stable. Romance fiction in the Philippines occupies an ever-changing terrain, with a myriad of influences: local and global, material and technological, emotional and practical.

In this chapter, we focus more closely on this Element's central case study – the community of authors, readers, artists, and actors known as #RomanceClass, who create, produce, and consume distinctly Filipino romance novels written in English – and examine how they navigate this terrain. We take as our starting point the notion that '[a] genre world is a social entity defined by interaction between its participants' (Fletcher *et al.*, 2018: 1008). The sociality of #RomanceClass is key to the way it is positioned within and steers through the Filipino romance literary landscape. We have written extensively elsewhere of the emotional and affective nature of the relationships in #RomanceClass, which regularly self-describes as a found family (McAlister *et al.*, 2020). Here, however, we focus on #RomanceClass as a professional entity. By banding together as a self-publishing collective which performs some functions of (but is not) a micro-publisher, members are able to carve out a distinct niche for themselves in a market dominated by Tagalog romance and books which originated on Wattpad.

#RomanceClass has two intertwined key features. The first is the way that community members regularly occupy multiple roles in the publishing process. The second is an ethos of care, both for each other and for the Filipino reader. The second has led them to innovate through mobilisation of the first. Where they have identified gaps or holes in the landscape of the Filipino romance landscape – whether practical, emotional, ideological, or of some other kind – they have sought to fill them so as to best serve Filipino romance readers (a category in which they include themselves). Additionally, while their focus remains firmly on the production of Filipino romance for a Filipino audience, their collectivity has enabled them to reach English-language readers outside the Philippines in a way that has not been possible for the vast majority of Filipino romance authors and novels in the past, even with the affordances of transnational platforms like Wattpad. They operate in both the local terrain of the Filipino romance market and the global terrain of the English-language romance market dominated by North America. In both terrains, they have a distinct brand imbued with a distinct meaning. The #RomanceClass logo on a book promises a certain kind of textual experience, but it also comes with guarantees about the way the book was produced: that multiple community members were involved in the process, that said process is professionalised, and that collective care (as distinct from capitalist churn) was involved in all steps along the way.

3.1 Context and Origins

In *The Philippines Is Not a Small Country*, Gideon Lasco claims that it is a 'futile endeavor' to 'comprehensively describe Philippines' national experience' given the complexity of the nation's social, economic, and political conditions (2020: xi). One essay in this book is pointedly entitled 'Failure of Empathy', detailing a phenomenon he describes as the failure 'to look after each other': the timeless refusal 'to consider one another as belonging to one and the same community' (Lasco, 2020: 32). Often summed up by the statement 'to each his own', this made occupation and colonisation of the country relatively easy, Lasco argues, since 'we fought not as one but as many' (Lasco, 2020: 32–3). He ties this phenomenon directly to a macro political context, arguing that an 'I am not one of them' mentality allowed many Filipino people to look away from political violence, from the martial law killings of journalists, activists, and political enemies during Ferdinand Marcos Sr's regime (1965–86) to the rampant extrajudicial killings during Rodrigo Duterte's implementation of the bloody war on drugs campaign (2016–22), mostly directed against the poor (2020: 33). However, we can also use it to look at the more micro context of the local traditional publishing industry, where – as discussed in previous chapters – the market is deeply segmented and where the financial bottom line is prioritised above all else.

The local trade bookselling ecosystem is a good example of this. There are major entanglements between publishers and booksellers, with financial considerations far outweighing any ideological notions of supporting local stories. For example, the English-language publisher Anvil (including the imprint Bliss Books, which publishes YA and romance works drawn from Wattpad) is a subsidiary of National Bookstore, the Philippines' premiere book chain. This has obvious implications for what books get stocked and where – and thus their sales. As Karryl Kim Abella Sagun and Brendan Luyt note in their discussion of the Filipino comics industry, local creators must deal with a myriad of intersecting challenges when seeking distribution: 'the high discounts that bookstores demand for books to be displayed on their shelves, [. . .] deficiency in government support and the lack of valuation for [local] cultural works' (2020: 109). This last challenge is particularly notable. The Philippine book market has long been seen as an extension of the US market, with imported books far exceeding exported ones (Anderson, 2016b). The market conditions – which also include high paper costs and heavy taxes on local books – are so challenging that Karina Bolasco reported to the Frankfurt Book Fair that '[i]n terms of book production, the Philippines is lagging behind most nations in the Asia-Pacific region; in fact, per capita it comes in last in the world' (Anderson, 2016b).

It is against this publishing landscape – which Mina V. Esguerra described as 'more about following numbers and stats than the story itself' (RomanceClass, 2020) – that #RomanceClass arose. As described in Chapter 1, Esguerra, the originator of the community, had several books traditionally published by Summit but became frustrated by the slow speed and low output, especially because her works and the works of authors like her were often deprioritised in favour of instant Wattpad hits. Therefore, she began to supplement her output with self-publishing (interview; see also De Vera, 2015). In 2013, she made a popular suggestion on Twitter that she start a 'romance class', where she would teach how to outline and write a book and then set a deadline so a group of writers could work together towards putting together a manuscript (interview). She created a Facebook group, which about a hundred people joined, many of whom were already known to Esguerra (interview). At the end of the six-month class, sixteen participants had developed full contemporary romance manuscripts. Esguerra tried to garner interest from local publishers but found it difficult in the Wattpad-dominated market for contemporary Filipino chick lit (interview). Therefore, #RomanceClass turned into a kind of 'self-publishing support group', with people editing for each other, discussing common issues, and working through the publishing process together (interview).

The ethos of collectivity and care that #RomanceClass has developed is in reaction to the local trade market. In her interview with us, Esguerra remarked that someone had suggested to her that the next step for #RomanceClass would be to formally become a publisher, something which she roundly rejected as incompatible with how the community operates, using the difficulty of distribution in the local market as an example:

> I mean the fight to get into a book store, it's not a victory, even if you get in because they don't necessarily care about the kind of books we're writing and if it comes down to a numbers game all over again, we'll lose the bookshelf space to somebody more popular because that's what they do, and *that's what we're trying not to do.* (Interview, our emphasis)

Rather than position themselves as a publisher, where a few very popular books might subsidise others (Esguerra, interview), #RomanceClass rejects this individualistic popularity-based metric in favour of a more community-minded approach which values many different kinds of local stories: antithetical to both the dominant ethos in local trade publishing and Lasco's 'failure to empathise'.

3.2 The Community

Esguerra still runs the titular romance classes, which take place entirely online so as not to disadvantage potential participants from outside Manila. The main content of the classes has moved from Facebook to email – Esguerra notes that the Facebook algorithm, which privileges engagement over chronology, made the platform unsuitable as people kept losing their place in the class – but the structure remains similar, as Esguerra takes participants through lectures and discussions on concept, outline, and a three-act structure (interview). If they keep pace with the class, then at the end – six months in the original class, now a maximum of three months – they should have a completed manuscript (interview). The lessons have also been compiled into a textbook, available on Gumroad for US$15, which promises to help users:

1. Learn a simple plot structure for a romance novella.
2. Set a reasonable and practical writing schedule.
3. Finish the manuscript and prepare it for publication. (Esguerra, 2022)

Not all of the #RomanceClass community members have their romance-writing origins in the classes. Bianca Mori (a pseudonym), for instance, was, like Esguerra, a traditionally published chick lit author, with several books published in the 2000s with Filipino press Psicom under the name Katrina Ramos Atienza. She had an existing relationship with Esguerra and reached out to her in 2013, as she was dissatisfied with the push her books were getting from her publisher and wanted assistance with self-publishing. By happenstance, this was concurrent with the first romance class and, in Mori's words, 'Mina started inviting me to events and that's how I met all these wonderful people' (de Guzman, Mori, Tan & Tanjutco, interview). She now publishes with #RomanceClass as Bianca Mori (with one story in a #RomanceClass anthology as Atienza). Similarly, Layla Tanjutco and Tania Arpa both had pre-existing relationships with Esguerra which became professional before the beginning of #RomanceClass. Tanjutco was a college friend who became Esguerra's editor, while Arpa and Esguerra were colleagues who went on to co-host a podcast before Arpa started designing Esguerra's covers (de Guzman, Mori, Tan & Tanjutco, interview; Arpa, interview). Both still perform these professional roles – they are, according to Esguerra, 'the key people that I work with' in her authorial career (interview) – but have gone on to perform other key roles in the #RomanceClass community: Tanjutco as one of the community's main editors – 'Layla edits everyone', one author told us – and as the make-up artist at the cover photo shoots (de Guzman, Mori, Tan, & Tanjutco, interview); and Arpa as a cover designer, author website designer, and producer and editor of the #RomanceClass podcast (Arpa, interview).

However, Mori, Tanjutco, and Arpa are exceptions rather than the rule. The majority of #RomanceClass members have come to the community through the classes. They came from different backgrounds and through different paths: Carla de Guzman, for instance, began in fan fiction before being connected to #RomanceClass while trying to work out how to self-publish one of her first original books. At the time, she told us, 'I didn't know anything about romance' but, after taking the class, has become one of the community's most prolific authors (de Guzman, Mori, Tan & Tanjutco, interview). Six de los Reyes joined a class after encountering a #RomanceClass booth at an indie event and has now published five books with them and contributed to two anthologies; while Danice P. Sison lurked in the #RomanceClass Facebook group after discovering it via Esguerra's blog before attempting the class in 2016 and ultimately succeeding in producing a manuscript in the 2017 class, which was focused on YA romance fiction (de los Reyes & Sison, vox pop interview). Some other authors, including Brigitte Bautista, Chi Yu Rodriguez, and Tara Frejas (the two latter of whom also began their writing careers with fan fiction), came to #RomanceClass via the #SparkNA workshop, run collaboratively between Esguerra and local publisher Anvil, who were looking for new adult contemporary romances for their Spark imprint (interviews). This workshop functioned in a way not dissimilar to the romance classes: it 'ran for six weeks, and [. . .] we need to finish the manuscript in that time, and then if we get selected we get the chance to be published by the local publisher [Anvil]' (Bautista, interview). Several #RomanceClass authors ultimately had books traditionally published in the Spark imprint but have continued their publishing journeys with #RomanceClass rather than with Anvil or other traditional publishers. For instance, Bautista's first book, *Don't Tell My Mother*, was published by Spark. She pitched her second book, *You, Me, U.S.*, to Anvil, as well as to international publishers but ultimately decided to self-publish with #RomanceClass after getting editorial feedback that would have taken the book in a very different direction to the one she wanted – something which also demonstrates #RomanceClass's ethos of care, here applied to the author's vision for the book (Bautista, interview).

At the time of writing, the #RomanceClass website lists ninety-seven authors. Since the first class in 2013, distinct guidelines for what a #RomanceClass book is have been established – among other things, it must have a central romance plot, it must end happily, and all sex must be 'consensual, responsible, and hot' (RomanceClass, n.d.a). The ways in which these guidelines overlap with and/or set #RomanceClass books apart from other kinds of Filipino romance have been discussed in Chapter 1. Of most interest for the purposes of this chapter, however, is the requirement that all #RomanceClass books:

> must have involved the romanceclass community in its publishing process, either through beta reader or sensitivity reader feedback that is actually responded to and addressed in the manuscript, or by contracting editors within the community or have worked on several romanceclass books. (RomanceClass, n.d.a)

This is expanded on in the media kit on the #RomanceClass website, which emphasises the fact that collective production and community feedback are fundamental to their publication process. It sets out a step-by-step guide for the publication of #RomanceClass books:

1. Manuscript is written.
2. Manuscript is read + commented on by romanceclass readers.
3. Book is edited.
4. Book is published in digital and print formats.
5. Readers find + read + share the book (media kit).

There is no passing from the first to the third step without the second. As Bianca Mori put it, for any given #RomanceClass book, 'it's important that many eyes see it before it goes off to the wild' (de Guzman, Mori, Tan & Tanjutco, interview). If a book bears the #RomanceClass logo, then it signifies that it will give the reader 'a consistent experience across different authors and different books' and that it will '[represent] what the community stands for' (Esguerra, 2020b). The branding contains a particular promise, much in the way that the branding of Harlequin Mills & Boon carries promises of typicality and equivalence (Fletcher *et al.*, 2019: 6). Part of the promise is textual: as discussed in Chapter 2, the reader knows what kind of experience they will be getting, what ideals will be upheld, and which boundaries will never be transgressed (see also McAlister *et al.*, 2020). This is intertwined with the second part of the promise. Despite the fact that the books are self-published – generally imagined as a very solitary endeavour, with the author taking on all roles usually performed by a publishing house – the other part of this promise is collectivity. If it takes a village to raise a child, here it takes a community to publish a book – which is why the first part of the promise, about the texts themselves and the kind of experience the reader can rely on, can be made in the first place.

Although Esguerra remains the central node of and main spokesperson for the #RomanceClass community, there is no requirement that every book pass through her hands: 'I trust a lot of the people with understanding what we're all doing', she told us (interview). Labour is shared throughout the community, and useful skills are pooled. As Esguerra told us: 'It's not a 24-hour operation for any one of us, but someone . . . I guess that was the key, someone volunteers the thing that they know how to do, but they also happen to understand what we're doing' (interview).

This means that within the community, members regularly occupy a variety of different roles. It is relatively rare for someone to be just an author or just a reader. Esguerra, of course, is author, teacher, organiser, and general coordinator, but others wear just as many hats. Miles Tan, for instance, does book cover design, layout design, and website design as well as being an author, describing herself to us as 'tech support' and an 'all around person' who also helps with things like assisting new authors in uploading ePub files to Amazon (de Guzman, Mori, Tan & Tanjutco, interview). Chi Yu Rodriguez is an author, has an established beta reader relationship with fellow author Brigitte Bautista, and is the photographer at the regular stock photo shoots for #RomanceClass covers (Rodriguez, interview). Tara Frejas is #RomanceClass's social media manager as well as one of their authors (Frejas, interview). These are only a few examples of many: it is extremely common for members of #RomanceClass to play multiple roles in the community.

Indeed, this collectivity is key to both the appeal of the community to members and their external branding. Intertwined with this is the community's ethos of care. This labour- and skill-sharing is a key way in which community members care for each other, but by using a collective lens and making sure books pass through many hands, with the checks and balances that entails, they are also able to provide care for the (presumed Filipino) reader. This is exhibited in almost everything #RomanceClass does, but we discuss two specific examples below: their frequent production of anthologies and their ongoing cover stock photo project.

3.3 Collectivity and Care Case Study 1: Anthologies

One natural result of #RomanceClass's collectivity is their frequent production of anthologies of romantic short stories. These anthologies will generally be curated by one or more community members; feature stories from several authors; and be beta-read, sensitivity-read, and/or edited by community members in the same way a book by a sole author would. Some of these anthologies feature a small number of authors. For example, at Feels Fest 2019, the #RomanceClass event we attended, the anthology *Alta: A High Society Romance Anthology* (2019) was launched, featuring stories from Bianca Mori, Carla de Guzman, and Suzette de Borja. Each story features a different set of romantic protagonists, but one member of each couple belongs to the 'filthy rich Aritz family', and the central action takes place against the backdrop of the Aritz matriarch's ninetieth birthday (Mori *et al.*, 2019). Other anthologies might include upwards of ten or fifteen authors. Such anthologies usually have a theme and/or a shared setting: they are not just disparate stories that community authors have happened to find a home for but are deliberately prepared for a particular anthology project. For instance, the 2017 anthology *Make My Wish Come True* is Christmas-themed and features seventeen stories by #RomanceClass authors (Tejano *et al.*, 2017). This includes stories by all three *Alta* authors, which provides a neat example of the relative frequency of anthology production in the community, in that authors contribute to them fairly frequently. These kinds of collective publications are much more common in #RomanceClass than they are in the broader North American–dominated English-language romance industry. They are also vastly more common than in traditional publishing, Filipino or otherwise, where anthologies are rarely viewed as a money-making proposition.

We interviewed several of the authors who contributed to *Make My Wish Come True*. They credited fellow community member Ana Tejano with being the brains behind the anthology: 'Ana Tejano brought up the idea of having a Christmas anthology and sent out a feeler on her Facebook group on who wants to join and basically most of us wanted to ... just basically Ana facilitated the whole thing', Miles Tan told us (de Guzman, Mori, Tan & Tanjutco, interview). However, while Tejano is listed as one of the anthology authors, the #RomanceClass website does not list her – or anyone – in a curatorial and/or editorial capacity. Similarly, in the book itself, the copyright page notes that she compiled the anthology, and she is thanked in the acknowledgements alongside a few other community members (including editor Rix Forto and cover designer Miles Tan) for 'putting this collection together' (Tejano *et al.*, 2017: loc. 5070), but there is no further acknowledgement of her curatorial and editorial work: for instance, she is not named as editor on the cover. This is common to most of the #RomanceClass anthologies, which list the contributing authors rather than foregrounding editorial curation: something which reinforces the community's emphasis on collectivity, the group privileged over the individual. It was the village that produced the book, not one person alone.

One notable exception to this is *Start Here*, a 2018 anthology which features exclusively LGBTQ+ romantic stories – it is 'unapologetically queer, happy endings required, with a smattering of that signature #romanceclass kilig' (RomanceClass, n.d.b). In this case, the contributions of editors Brigitte Bautista and Ronald Lim, two of #RomanceClass's openly LGBTQ+ authors, were foregrounded on the cover, with an 'edited by' label appearing under the names of the authors. Within the book itself, there is an 'about the editors' as well as an 'about the authors' section, and it opens with a sort of foreword entitled 'Hey, Start Here', where Bautista and Lim set out their vision for the anthology. Lim writes:

> I never got those stories [romantic stories with queer Filipino leads getting a happy ending] when I was young, but that doesn't mean today's young gay, lesbian, or non-binary kids can't get those stories now. Here they get their kisses in the moonlight, their New York romances, their

passionate lovemaking after being soaked in the rain. Here, in some small way, maybe we can make their life easier. (Lim & Bautista, 2018: 46–53)

The implied reader here – in both senses of the term as described by Wolf Schmid, 'presumed addressee' and 'ideal recipient' (2013) – is a queer Filipino reader, probably a young one. The care expressed for this reader is explicit: the desire to 'make their life easier'. Bautista expresses something similar in her contribution to the foreword, where she writes:

> Being queer in this country isn't exactly the easiest life. When LGBT+ people can't even be protected from discrimination, the daily grind can get too exhausting at times. The endings aren't always happy; the encounters not always worth remembering.
>
> This anthology flips the script, throws it on its side. It celebrates. It uplifts. It inspires. In a world where our experiences are so often underrepresented or misrepresented, these stories put queer characters front and center. Their personalities, decisions, conflicts and endings are written with care and respect. (Lim & Bautista, 2018: 53–9)

The unusually clear identification of *Start Here*'s editors is, we contend, a demonstration of this care and respect. The term #OwnVoices, first coined by Dutch author Corinne Duyvis, refers to work portraying characters of minority backgrounds written by authors of those backgrounds. In the case of *Start Here*, not all the authors were #OwnVoices when it came to LGBTQ representation, but the two editors were. By identifying Lim and Bautista's contributions clearly in the volume's paratext, it communicated to the implied reader that they were in safe hands – another example of #RomanceClass's ethos of care.

This ethos is even more bluntly demonstrated in some of #RomanceClass's more recent anthologies, *The Tropetastic Kindness Bundle* and *NomCom: Tropetastic Kindness Bundle 2* (Tejano *et al.*, 2022), where all the proceeds are donated to charity: Filipina feminist publisher Gantala Press and two charities focusing on education and literacy for vulnerable communities in the Philippines for the former, and a youth-led organisation that helps Filipino farmers for the latter. These two bundles were published exclusively on Gumroad, a platform which enables 'name a fair price' as a payment option. The suggested price points were modest – US$7 for the second one – but this option allowed buyers the option of donating substantially more money to the given charities. Interestingly, both bundles were limited-time-only offers: at the time of writing, the second bundle is still available but the first bundle has been unpublished. Some authors have republished their stories in other venues, such as Wattpad, but others have not, and they are no longer available anywhere as a collection (despite the fact they have shared settings: the fictional St Tropez Court condominium in Ortigas for the first bundle and the fictional NomNom Commons Food Park, also in Ortigas, for the second). The exclusivity of the limited-time offer allowed the community to raise more money for their chosen local charities than they might otherwise have been able to with perpetual availability; however, this limited-time offer also runs counter to most conventional wisdom about self-publishing, which emphasises the importance and power of the backlist for authors as a form of brand recognition. The authors can now do with the stories what they like, including potentially publishing them in a place where they might make money from them. However, this is hardly a lucrative opportunity, especially for individual stories divorced from the broader shared universe of the bundle. This shows how markedly different some of #RomanceClass's priorities can be from traditional publishers and even other self-published authors. Its collectivity and ethos of care sometimes manifest in ways which seem entirely counter-intuitive when viewed through the lens of the neoliberal marketplace of the publishing industry, traditional and independent, local and global.

3.4 Collectivity and Care Case Study 2: Cover Shoots

'All we wanted was to see our faces on the covers of our books', #RomanceClass author Carla de Guzman writes in an article for romance-centric media site Frolic. 'It sounds like a simple premise, but at the time, it was a complicated thing' (de Guzman, 2019).

This is one of the key problems that #RomanceClass has worked together as a collective to solve: how do you signal to your target audience via your covers what your books are? In the case of #RomanceClass, authors want to signal that their books are a) romance novels and b) feature Filipino characters – as community member and photographer Chi Yu Rodriguez puts it, '[w]e want our books to scream "Romance! Filipino!" with very little explanation' (Rodriguez, 2019). The obvious solution is to use Filipino models in romantic poses on the covers; however, as Mina Esguerra writes, '[t]here just aren't enough cover-worthy romance stock photos with Filipinos (or Asians even), or at least not enough for all the stories we've been writing' (Esguerra, 2016). In order to solve this problem, #RomanceClass has an ongoing project where members pool resources, both financial and skill-based, and do stock photo shoots featuring local actors. Many photos from these shoots have gone on to be the covers of #RomanceClass novels; however, they are also for sale more broadly, in the hope that more Filipino and/or Asian authors writing Filipino and/or Asian characters will be able to see their characters represented accurately and authentically on their covers (Esguerra, 2016).

There are practical reasons behind this desire to see Filipino faces on book covers, the most basic one being the desire to hail local readers in a market flooded by overseas imports. But there are (arguably more important) ideological reasons as well, linked to the community's ethos of care. Various community members use different phrases to express this, but the meaning is essentially the same. In Rodriguez's words, it is important to the community to see 'our stories depicted on book covers, with faces we see in our everyday lives as Filipinos' (2019). In de Guzman's, '[i]t was time to see ourselves in the books we wrote' (2019). And in Esguerra's, it 'is a soul-enriching experience, to see Filipinos on romance book covers. It's wonderful for the author, for readers, and even for the cover models we invite, many of them surprised to be told they could be a Main Character or Love Interest' (2019).

It is no secret that romance fiction, like publishing more broadly, has historically been dominated by white stories – a phenomenon that Claire Squires calls 'publishing's diversity deficit' (2017). According to the racial diversity report published by the Ripped Bodice (2016; 2017; 2018; 2019; 2020) a romance-specialist bookstore based in Los Angeles, as of 2020, only

12 out of every 100 romance novels published by the major traditional romance publishers were written by an author who was Black, Indigenous, or a person of colour (compared with 8.3 in 2019, 7.7 in 2018, 6.2 in 2017, and 7.8 in 2016). While this report is by no means exhaustive and its methodology is unclear, and it encompasses only traditional publishing, it indicates the extent to which romance fiction is still hugely dominated by white authors, white characters, and white perspectives. This filters through to the implied readership – as we have written elsewhere, there is 'an implicit supposition that the default protagonists and readers [of romance fiction] are white, middle-class, and usually American' (McAlister *et al.*, 2020: 3). The end result is the reinforcement of an attitude that this specific group are the ones deserving of love and of being centred in narratives about love. To use a blunt 'if you can't see it, you can't be it' approach, if a reader never sees someone like them in a certain narrative position – here, in Esguerra's terms, 'Main Character or Love Interest' (2019) – then there is a strong chance that it will lead to them assuming that they cannot occupy this position. The broader project of #RomanceClass – that is, producing romance novels featuring Filipino leads, usually also set in the Philippines – explicitly troubles the assumptions inherent in the mainstream white- and North American–dominated romance industry, but this is perhaps nowhere more visible than in the covers. By creating these covers, the community are demonstrating that Filipino people can be and are romantic protagonists. Because of this, the covers project is explicitly framed through a lens of care by the community. As Rodriguez says, 'we want more people to feel seen as deserving of their own happily ever after . . . both on the cover and behind it' (2019).

The concept behind the #RomanceClass covers project is thus relatively clear. However, as de Guzman noted in our interview, while it seems simple on the surface, it has required a reasonably complex collective solution to be able to undertake the project successfully. Like many #RomanceClass initiatives, it began with Mina Esguerra. As she began to hybridise her authorial career, moving more into the global world of self-publishing and away from the local world of traditional publishing in the Philippines, she found her covers were out of step with international standards: as she told us, 'when I was published here, the standard was illustrated cover in the manner of chick-lit, vector, heart, pink [. . .] but when I was publishing for Amazon, it looked out of place with other romance books of the same age group' (interview). She and her cover designer Tania Arpa began to use stock photos of dark-haired women who could potentially be read as Filipina (interview) and also to collaborate with local style bloggers, where they predominantly purchased pre-existing photos from their portfolios (Esguerra, 2014). This built to the first ever #RomanceClass photo shoot, featuring models Katrice Kierulf and Migs Almendras, shot in several different outfits, which formed the basis of the first #RomanceClass catalogue of cover stock photos (Esguerra, interview). Authors could purchase an image from this catalogue, with pricing dependent on use – for example, photos were available in web quality or print quality, non-exclusively or exclusively.

Esguerra and her photographer sponsored the first shoot (interview), but the first catalogue also came with the option 'to sponsor a shoot for more perks and to get the look you want' (Esguerra, 2016). #RomanceClass cover shoots are now 'co-sponsored' by a few authors at a time (Esguerra, 2017b). This is a classic example of how #RomanceClass operates as a professionalised collective. Financial resources are pooled by the authors, in order to pay for studio time, models, and other associated expenses. Skills are also pooled: for example, Rodriguez is the photographer, Esguerra does most of the liaising with models, Tanjutco does the make-up, and authors are often on set as well. 'It's really a collaborative effort', writes de Guzman (2019). She has first-hand experience of playing multiple roles in the cover design process. Not only does she design many of her own book covers, using shots from #RomanceClass cover shoots, but she has also appeared as a model on the cover of one of her own books, *If the Dress Fits* (2017), alongside local actor Jef Flores.

If the Dress Fits is a neat example of how #RomanceClass shoots have largely come to work. While they still shoot generic catalogue shots, predominantly shoots are set up and models are cast for specific books – as photographer Rodriguez puts it, 'most of our stuff in Romance Class covers gets sponsored, so if someone needs a certain look for a certain cover, we do that and they pay for that and then we do the shoot' (interview). The community has established relationships with several local actors who perform regularly in their live reading events as well as their audio and video material (also excellent demonstrations of the community's professionalised collectivity and ethos of care that we do not have the space to address fully here but have discussed at length elsewhere: see McAlister *et al.*, 2020; Parnell *et al.*, 2021a; Parnell *et al.*, 2021b). These actors regularly appear on #RomanceClass covers – like Flores on *If the Dress Fits* – but they are not the sole pool for models. Because a lot of the shoots are sponsored, models are now cast to fit a specific type. *If the Dress Fits* has a plus-size heroine, and so – after much encouragement from fellow community members – de Guzman modelled for it herself (de Guzman, Mori, Tan & Tanjutco, interview). Similarly, for the book *Raya and Grayson's Guide to Saving the World* by Catherine Dellosa (2019), which is a YA romance, the actor portraying Grayson needed to be Chinese Filipino and to fit the character's age bracket. It took a while to find a suitable model, but they succeeded eventually, something which Esguerra links to a broader discussion in North American–dominated publishing about the difficulty of finding the right models to be on photographic book covers. '[P]eople who have more resources are saying they can't find specific body types, specific models, specific ethnicities', she told us. 'I mean it's not impossible. Not at all' (interview).

This links back to the central motivation of the covers project, which is to explicitly feature Filipino romantic protagonists. Increasingly, the covers and books have symbiotically developed in order to complicate this. There is a commitment not just to representing Filipino people as romantic leads but also to representing diversity within this group – that is, to not representing Filipino people as a monolith. This is not a simple case of covers representing increased diversity within the texts but rather of the covers project allowing authors to feel supported in writing more diverse protagonists. For instance, as Esguerra told us in regard to the representation of plus-sized characters:

> I think it [the collective cover shoots] also encourages the other authors to write plus-size because they will be supported in the publishing back end, like it's okay – because sometimes it's so interesting how people decide when they

know that they won't get support; sometimes they just will decide the easy way – if they know that the support system is in place for their success, then they'll just do that. So here, it's kind of like ... here we're encouraging them to think that it's okay to write this character. (Interview)

Above, we discussed the ways in which the covers project demonstrates the community's ethos of care for the implied reader, who can see themselves represented on covers in a way that has hitherto not been possible. Here, though, we can also see the ethos of care for the writer. By providing this collective infrastructure, #RomanceClass allows its authors to explore and experiment in a way that they might not otherwise have felt possible. This is typical of the #RomanceClass community – as Rodriguez writes:

The Cliffs Notes version of it [i.e. where the covers project came from] is that we needed something that wasn't being made available to us, so we just did the thing and made it available ourselves. (Which is a running theme with us over here at #RomanceClass). (2019)

This is a neat example of the ways in which the community's distinctive collectivity and care are intertwined: the collectivity *is* care. We have written elsewhere about how this works in terms of the community's emotional support of each other (McAlister *et al.*, 2020). What the covers project shows is that this is also professionalised, as the community works together to provide each other with infrastructure that they would not have access to on their own, in a way which encourages their authorial growth (see Parnell *et al.*, 2021a for how live readings perform similar work).

Notably, this infrastructure can, in some ways, surpass that made available by traditional publishers. One #RomanceClass author, Carla de Guzman, has had books published by major North American romance imprint Carina. Both *Sweet on You* (2020) and *A Match Made in Lipa* (2022) – romances set in the Philippines featuring Filipino characters – feature cover images from #RomanceClass shoots.

3.5 Conclusion

Romance fiction is often discussed in terms of volume and mass production (Fletcher *et al.*, 2019). This is inherently linked with capitalist publishing logics in order to make a case for romance's worth. The fact that romance is a 'billion-dollar industry' is liberally cited in order to make a case for its worth (an extremely non-exhaustive list of examples: Haupt, 2021; Leach, 2019; Lit Hub, 2020; Swartz, 2020; Valby, 2014). Claims along these lines are frequently repeated by major romance industry bodies. For instance, at the time of writing, the Romance Writers of America refer to romance as a billion-dollar industry on the homepage of their website (RWA, n.d.). Similarly, major romance publisher Harlequin Mills & Boon frequently repeat the claim that their books are sold at a rate of one every x seconds (the precise number changes between territories and sources – for more on this, see Fletcher *et al.*, 2019). This phenomenon is not limited to the North American–dominated romance marketplace – as Jurilla notes in her landmark study of the history of the book in the Philippines, 'the most important aspect of the Filipino romance novel publishing business [is that] it was intensely market driven' (2008: 169).

However, #RomanceClass rarely invokes this kind of rhetoric. In an industry often discussed in terms of how much money it makes and how many books it produces, they almost never talk about questions of quantity at all. Jurilla notes that the number of editions printed of a book, as opposed to the number of copies, is generally the way a book's performance in the market is measured in the Philippines, but in our interviews of, fieldwork in, and study around #RomanceClass, this wasn't really mentioned either. The community priorities are very obviously different.

This is not to say that #RomanceClass are not savvy operators within the local and global romance industries, because they clearly are. As discussed above, their collective infrastructure gives them opportunities and possibilities that they might not otherwise have. Chief among these is visibility: as a distinctly branded unit, they are far more visible than they might have been otherwise. This is particularly true on the international level, where their works have penetrated the market in a way that other Filipino romance authors (particularly those writing in Tagalog and other

Filipino languages) have not been able to. Print editions of #RomanceClass books are stocked by the Ripped Bodice. Carla de Guzman has had two books published by Carina Press. Mina V. Esguerra has spoken about #RomanceClass in several international venues (including the International Association for the Study of Popular Romance conference in Sydney in 2018, which was ultimately the impetus for this academic project). Articles by #RomanceClass authors have been published in international media outlets such as Frolic. While their implied reader is Filipino and the Philippines remains their core audience base, they have readers in the United States, Canada, Australia, United Kingdom, Brazil, India, Saudi Arabia, Japan, Qatar, Singapore, Germany, New Zealand, Mexico, and Tanzania (non-exhaustive – this was their top fifteen countries of readership during our fieldwork in 2019, according to Miles Tan, who tracks these statistics for the community; de Guzman, Mori, Tan & Tanjutco, interview).

Their professionalised collectivity thus has clear career benefits for the authors involved, but it does not appear to be the draw or the appeal of #RomanceClass for the community. Nor is it the point. Some of their decisions seem strange when viewed through the typical neoliberal lens of the publishing industry, such as removing their charity bundles from sale after a specific period of time, or capping event attendance at fifty, which they did at the event we attended in October 2019. However, when one considers the centrality of care to the community, things come into sharper focus. The one-sentence description on their website describes them as 'a community of writers, readers, actors, and artists who gather together to do what we love'. Nearly every community member we spoke to talked about the community in deeply affective, emotional terms (McAlister *et al.*, 2020). In an industry enormously driven by mass, volume, quantity, and money, #RomanceClass has reprioritised. By doing so collectively, it has incorporated some of the key emotional drivers of romance fiction – love, joy, hope, care – into the publishing process itself.

Conclusion: Decentralising Romance Fiction

In this Element, we have explored the complex and multilayered genre world of Filipino romance fiction. As we have shown, the publishing ecosystem in the Philippines is deeply complicated: in some areas fragmented, with different forms of romance fiction reaching almost entirely different audiences; in some areas entangled, with publishers, platforms, distribution networks, and other aspects of the industry enmeshed with each other. Our central case study, #RomanceClass, has developed against the backdrop of this local ecosystem, with many of their key practices functioning as solutions to the problems posed by it, even as they also reach out into the broader international publishing landscape.

One of our key aims in doing this was to disrupt the perpetual focus on the Anglo-American publishing market, both in popular romance studies and in studies of literature and publishing more broadly. There have been many discussions, in industrial, writerly, readerly, and scholarly spaces, about popular romance fiction's 'overwhelming whiteness' (Jagodzinski, 2014: 2). This is aptly positioned as a problem, and there has been a concerted effort within the Anglo-American industry to address it. While this is, of course, a good thing, the perpetual centring of this dominant market also mirrors the ways in which the global North continually positions itself as a benevolent figure that charitably addresses the needs and wants of global South audiences. It thus maintains the dominance of the Anglo-American romance industry, positioning it as the institution which will serve 'the needs of its increasingly diverse and international audience' (Cassiday & Johnson, 2020: 1), rather than considering the ways in which some of these audiences can meet or are already meeting their own needs, as we see in the case of the Philippines.

This does not mean that we should understate the power and influence of the Anglo-American romance industry, which is clearly felt even in places like the Philippines, which have their own highly developed and distinctive romance publishing ecosystem. However, we should acknowledge that not all territories have 'an obvious lacuna in the romance market', just waiting for Anglo-American works in translation to fill (Cassiday & Johnson, 2020: 2). Rather, as popular romance studies develop further, we hope that our study of romance in the Philippines will be an early effort that takes a transnational approach, disrupting the hegemonic positioning of the dominant industry to recognise multiple and rhizomatic nodes in romance fiction's history and development. Examining how the genre is understood and configured outside the Anglo-American marketplace is key to this, positioning romance not as inherently Anglo-American, although willing to be enriched through participation from the 'other', but as a transnational literary form where this centre/margins dichotomy is complicated and collapsed in order to look at romance as a dislocated and decentred industrial, textual, and social phenomenon.

By focusing on the Philippines, this Element is thus an exercise in 're-territorializing' (Baudinette, 2020: 110) the romance genre's networked production, distribution, and consumption. This allows heterogeneous romance subjects (e.g. authors, publishers, readers) with various political and sociocultural positions to be understood on their own terms rather than through the lens of the hegemonic centre, examining how their knowledge systems and the ways they have developed over time create a distinct romance ecosystem. Folie neatly describes this way of looking at genre:

> View[ing] genres not as hierarchical 'trees,' with one common, usually monolingual and/or monocultural root, but rather as 'rhizomes' with multiple beginnings, might lead to pluralistic and interrelated literary herstories that have the potential to deepen our understanding of contemporary literary phenomena. (2020: 6)

Using this approach, romance fiction should therefore not be seen as a mere contribution handed by the centre to the margins through historical mechanisms such as colonisation, globalisation, or even digitalisation; but as something with a far more complex origin story, where genre develops in complex cultural contexts. In the Philippines, the nation's position as a postcolony where Western ideological forces are deeply felt through the continued imperialism of the United States has a marked effect on the layered tensions between the global and the local in its romance genre world. For instance, Soledad Reyes asserts that although nearly 90 per cent of early Filipino romance novels were patterned after the category romance novels of Mills & Boon, it is not reasonable to treat these texts primarily as local versions of Western romances (2001). Rather, she contends, these five-peso novels contain deeper material realities rooted in the obvious experience of socio-economic discrepancies in the country (Reyes, 2001): a neat example of how this transnational approach to romance fiction can recognise the impact of the Anglo-American industry while also understanding the local ecosystem on its own terms.

Complicating the Monolith

If the first of our key aims in this Element was to understand Filipino romance fiction in its own context, the second was to show that Filipino romance fiction is by no means a singular monolithic entity. It operates in different ways, in different languages and contexts, and serves different audiences. The Filipino romance publishing landscape is multistranded, in which networked industries, varied means of textual production, and numerous avenues for community formations around the genre converge (and, arguably, diverge). Moreover, it is deeply entangled with other kinds of media production. Katherine Morrissey argues for an understanding of 'romance' which is 'not simply the romance novel, but a broader cultural construct that appears in film, television, print, and digital media' (2014: 3). In the Philippines, it is difficult to approach romance in any other way.

The complicated nature of romance in the Philippines is epitomised in our case study, the self-publishing collective #RomanceClass. Mirroring the entangled local media production landscape discussed in Chapter 1 of this Element, the novels they produce are complemented by a host of other forms of multimedia artefacts, including live and digital events (Parnell *et al.*, 2021a) and audio-visual paratexts (such as the *Hello Ever After* epilogue web series – for more on this, see Parnell *et al.*, 2021b). As discussed in Chapter 2, their texts, which are in English, serve a particular part of the romance-reading audience in the Philippines and can also be read as a distinct alternative to other forms of local romance, such as Tagalog pocketbooks. Finally, as discussed in Chapter 3, their community practices and infrastructure have developed in large part to solve problems caused by and/or fill gaps in the local and global publishing ecosystems, ranging from the political (e.g. the relative lack of local queer romance) to the practical (e.g. the lack of stock photos for book covers featuring Filipino models). The result is a new form of romance fiction: one with ties to other local forms and to Anglo-American forms of romance, but one which is also highly distinctive of this community, making them an excellent example of Jagodzinski's description of romance as 'constantly reinvent[ing] itself while maintaining its core identity' (2014: 1).

#RomanceClass can be read as part of a project of decentralising romance in many ways. Firstly, looking outwards, as the first form of Filipino romance fiction to penetrate the Anglophone West in any kind of sustained way (abetted by the fact that it is in English), it contributes to the disruption of the Anglo-American norm. Secondly, looking inwards, it seeks to disrupt local hegemonies by depicting many different kinds of Filipino people, locations, and experiences.

This speaks directly to a long-term focus on decentring in the Filipino academe, which has been both primary witness to and part of the ideological apparatus for the ways in which economic and cultural projects are largely established in imperial Manila, the geographically advantageous place identified by the Spanish and American colonial governments for the centralisation of the country's leadership. Ideologies have also long been initiated and circulated from the local centre to the hyperlocal margins. From the chosen national language, Filipino, which is made up in large part of the Tagalog language vocabulary, to the idea of a national historiography and literary tradition, Manila as the centre has the tendency to dictate what knowledge is to be propagated throughout the entire archipelago as a representation of the country's collective history, literature, and popular culture. This form of centralisation has long been a problem which fails to encapsulate how multicultural the country is and how many multiple identities are covered by the term 'Filipino'. In this Element, through our explication of the complexities of the romance publishing ecosystem and the multiple audiences it serves, and our focus on #RomanceClass, which seeks to complicate and diversify representations of 'Filipino-ness', we hope we have contributed meaningfully to this project of decentring, looking both inwards and outwards.

References

Abdullah-Poulos, L. (2018). 'The Stable Muslim Love Triangle: Triangular Desire in African American Muslim Romance Fiction'. *Journal of Popular Romance Studies*, 7, https://bit.ly/3JWcGWu. Accessed 27 June 2022.

Abinales, P. (1981). 'The Concern with Literature'. *Book Publishing and Philippine Scholarship*, Manila: Published for Book Development Association of the Philippines by Daily Star Pub. Co.

ABS-CBN (2020). 'ABS-CBN, Most Watched Network Nationwide in 2019'. *ABS-CBN*, 8 January, www.abs-cbn.com/newsroom/tv-ratings/2020/1/8/abscbn-2019-ratings. Accessed 9 December 2022.

Adobo Magazine (2018). 'Wattpad Now Reaches Seven Million People in the Philippines Each Month'. *Adobo Magazine*, 2 May, https://bit.ly/3HO9HN5. Accessed 22 May 2022.

Alicante, K. (2007). *Then and Now*, Quezon City: Precious Pages Corporation.

Anderson, P. (2016a). 'Flirting With New Readers in the Philippines: Wattpad Presents'. *MediaShift*, 16 February, http://bit.ly/3I9tZls. Accessed 27 June 2022.

Anderson, P. (2016b). 'Frankfurt's The Markets: A Snapshot of the Philippines'. *Publishing Perspectives*, 31 May, http://bit.ly/3RQtL5R. Accessed 12 December 2022.

Anjani, L., Mok, T., Tang, A., Oehlberg, L. & Goh, W. B. (2020). 'Why Do People Watch Others Eat Food? An Empirical Study on the Motivations and Practices of Mukbang Viewers'. *Proceedings of the 2020 CHI Conference on Human Factors in Computing Systems*, https://doi.org/10.1145/3313831.3376567.

Aquino, A. (2003). *Drama Queen*, Manila: Summit Books.

Bach, E. (1997). 'Sheik Fantasies: Orientalism and Feminine Desire in the Desert Romance'. *Hecate*, 23(1), 9–40.

Balangue, M. D. (2003). *Mr. Write*, Manila: Summit Books.

Barrios, J. (2001). *Ang Aking Prince Charming At Iba Pang Noveleta Ng Pag-ibig*, Quezon City: University of the Philippines Press.

Baudinette, T. (2020). 'Creative Misreadings of "Thai BL" by a Filipino Fan Community: Dislocating Knowledge Production in Transnational Queer Fandoms Through Aspirational Consumption'. *Mechademia: Second Arc*, 13(1), 101–18.

Bautista, B. (2019). *You, Me, U.S.*, Manila: Brigitte Bautista.

Bautista, L. (1985). *Pag-ibig Ko, Karapatan Ko*, Quezon City: Books for Pleasure.

Becker, H. (1982). *Art Worlds*, Berkeley: University of California Press.

Bernardino, B. (2013). *She's Dating the Gangster*, Manila: Pop Fiction.

Bohidar, M. (2021). 'Performances of "Reel" and "Real" Lives: Negotiating Public Romance in Urban India'. In A. Brooks, ed., *The Routledge Companion to Romantic Love*, Abingdon: Routledge, pp. 239–50.

Bolisay, R. (2015). '"Yes, You Belong to Me!": Reflections on the JaDine Love Team Fandom in the Age of Twitter and in the Context of Filipino Fan Culture'. *Plaridel*, 12(1), 41–61.

Bookware Publishing Corporation (2022). 'About Us'. *Bookware Publishing*, www.bookwarepublishing.com/about/. Accessed 8 November 2022.

Buhain, A. D. D. (1998). *A History of Publishing in the Philippines*, Quezon City: Rex Book Store.

Burge, A. (2016). *Representing Difference in the Medieval and Modern Orientalist Romance: The New Middle Ages*, New York: Palgrave Macmillan.

Burge, A. & Folie, S. (2021). 'Girls of Riyadh and Desperate in Dubai: Reading and Writing Romance in the Middle East'. In A. Brooks, ed., *The Routledge Companion to Romantic Love*, Abingdon: Routledge, pp. 323–33.

Calica, M. (2003). *The Breakup Diaries*, Manila: Summit Books.

Cassiday, J. A. & Johnson, E. D. (2020). 'Special Issue: Romance Fiction in the International Marketplace (Editors' Introduction)'. *Journal of Popular Romance Studies*, 9, https://bit.ly/3Xep86F. Accessed 27 June 2022.

Constantino, R. (1970). 'The Mis-Education of the Filipino'. *Journal of Contemporary Asia*, 1(1), 20–36.

Cruz, M. E. (1985). *Kahit Mahal Kita*, Quezon City: Books for Pleasure.

Cuthbert, K. (2021). 'The Australian Digital Publishing Bubble, 2012–2016: An Insider Perspective'. In A. Dane & M. Weber, eds., *Post-Digital Book Cultures: Australian Perspectives*, Melbourne: Monash University Press, pp. 115–39.

Dandridge, R. B. (2010). 'The African American Historical Romance: An Interview with Beverly Jenkins'. *Journal of Popular Romance Studies*, 1 (1), https://bit.ly/3RTSKW8. Accessed 27 June 2022.

Dandridge, R. B. (2022). 'Vivian Lorraine Stephens: Romance Pioneer'. *Journal of Popular Romance Studies*, 11, https://bit.ly/3lmRcaP. Accessed 27 June 2022.

de Guzman, C. (2017). *If the Dress Fits*, Manila: Carla de Guzman.

de Guzman, C. (2018). *How She Likes It*, Manila: Carla de Guzman.

de Guzman, C. (2019). 'Behind The Scenes of a #Romanceclass Cover Shoot by Carla de Guzman'. *Frolic*, 14 August, https://bit.ly/3YAjRrg. Accessed 21 June 2022.

de Guzman, C. (2020). *Sweet on You*, Toronto: Carina Press.

de Guzman, C. (2022). *A Match Made in Lipa*, Toronto: Carina Press.

Deinla, I. & Dressel B. (2019). 'Introduction: From Aquino II to Duterte (2010–2018): Change, Continuity – and Rupture'. In I. Deinla & B. Dressel, eds., *From Aquino II to Duterte (2010–2018): Change, Continuity – and Rupture*, Singapore: ISEAS Publishing, pp. 1–36.

Dellosa, C. (2019). *Raya and Grayson's Guide to Saving the World*, Manila: Catherine Dellosa.

De Vera, R. S. (2015). 'The Romantic Empire of Mina V. Esguerra'. *Lifestyle Inq*, 19 January, https://bit.ly/3YoZVYH. Accessed 16 April 2022.

Driscoll, B., Fletcher, L., Wilkins, K. & Carter, D. (2018). 'The Publishing Ecosystems of Contemporary Australian Genre Fiction'. *Creative Industries Journal*, 11(2), 203–21.

Dumaual M. (2021). 'The Curious Case of "DonBelle": A Trending Love Team Even Before Its Launch'. *ABS-CBN*, 30 March, http://bit.ly/3YEzU7r. Accessed 30 May 2022.

Elam, D. (1992). *Romancing the Postmodern*, London: Routledge.

Ellis, J. (1982). 'The Literary Adaptation'. *Screen*, 23(1), 3–5.

Esguerra, M. V. (2014). 'Beautiful Collaborations: Fashion Bloggers and My Books'. *Mina V. Esguerra*, 19 May, http://bit.ly/3YzjVbn. Accessed 16 April 2022.

Esguerra, M. V. (2016). 'Romanceclasscovers: Romance-y Covers for Our Books'. *Mina V. Esguerra*, 10 April, https://bit.ly/3IbNjhS. Accessed 16 April 2022.

Esguerra, M. V. (2017a). *Better at Weddings Than You*, Manila: Bright Girl Books.

Esguerra, M. V. (2017b). '#romanceclasscovers, An Update'. *Mina V. Esguerra*, 10 September, https://minavesguerra.com/news/romance classcovers-an-update/. Accessed 16 April 2022.

Esguerra, M. V. (2018). *What Kind of Day*, Manila: Bright Girl Books.

Esguerra, M. V. (2019). '#romanceclasscovers Update: 9 and We'll Keep Going'. *Mina V. Esguerra*, 22 January, http://bit.ly/3IbUOFH. Accessed 16 April 2022.

Esguerra, M. V. (2020a). 'Heat Levels in RomanceClass'. *RomanceClass*, 17 February, https://bit.ly/3DV1zZU. Accessed 16 April 2022.

Esguerra, M. V. (2020b). 'About RomanceClass (2020 Update)'. *Mina V. Esguerra*, 2 November, https://minavesguerra.com/news/about-romanceclass-2020-update/. Accessed 16 April 2022.

Esguerra, M. (2022). '#romanceclass textbook'. *Gumroad*, n.d., https://mina vesguerra.gumroad.com/l/romanceclass. Accessed 22 February 2023.

Estella, P. G. R. & Löffelholz, M. (n.d.). 'Media Landscapes: Philippines'. *European Journalism Centre*, https://medialandscapes.org/country/philippines. Accessed 27 June 2022.

Evasco, M. M. (2002). 'Weekly Smorgasbord of Feminine Pleasures'. In S. Reyes, ed., *Reading Popular Culture*, Quezon City: Ateneo de Manila University Press, pp. 165–75.

Feng, J. (2021). 'Cook For A Better Life: The Economy of Food and Sex in Chinese Web Romance.' In A. Brooks, ed., *The Routledge Companion to Romantic Love*, London: Routledge, pp. 295–303.

Fermin, T. A. S. (2013). 'Appropriating Yaoi and Boys Love in the Philippines'. *EJCJS*, 13(3), http://japanesestudies.org.uk/ejcjs/vol13/iss3/fermin.html. Accessed 27 June 2022.

Fielding, H. (1996). *Bridget Jones's Diary*, London: Picador.

Fletcher, L., Driscoll, B. & Wilkins, K. (2018). 'Genre Worlds and Popular Fiction: The Case of Twenty-First-Century Australian Romance'. *Journal of Popular Culture*, 51(4), 997–1015.

Fletcher, L., McAlister, J., Temple, K. & Williams, K. (2019). '#love-yourshelfie: Mills & Boon Books and How to Find Them'. *Mémoires Du Livre/Studies in Book Culture*, 11(1), https://id.erudit.org/iderudit/1066945ar. Accessed 27 June 2022.

Folie, S. (2020). 'Review: Theorizing Ethnicity and Nationality in the Chick Lit Genre'. *Journal of Popular Romance Studies*, 9, https://bit.ly/415luiQ. Accessed 27 June 2022.

France-Presse, A. (2011). '"Conservative" Romance Novels Attract Poor Filipinos: UCA News'. *Ucanews.Com*, 24 August, http://bit.ly/3S5aU7o. Accessed 12 April 2022.

Gonzales, A. (2004). 'The Social Dimensions of Philippine English'. *World Englishes*, 23(1), 7–16.

Haupt, A. (2021). 'How the Romance Genre Found Its Happily Ever After'. *Washington Post*, 15 April, http://bit.ly/3jZo0Xf. Accessed 27 June 2022.

Hendricks, M. (2022). 'Against Odds: Beverly Jenkins' Indigo and Black Historical Romance'. *Journal of Popular Romance Studies*, 11, https://bit.ly/3I8cr86. Accessed 27 June 2022.

Hendricks, M. & Moody-Freeman J. E. (2022). 'Introduction to the Special Issue on Black Romance'. *Journal of Popular Romance Studies*, 11, https://bit.ly/415naZG. Accessed 27 June 2022.

Heruela, A., Gonzales, G. & Reyles, Q. (2015). 'Mandie Lee'. In Q. Reyles, ed., *25 Most Precious*, Quezon City: Precious Pages Corporation, pp. 138–43.

Huguley, P. (2022). 'Her Bodyguard: Sandra Kitt's *The Color of Love* as a Foundational Text for BWWM Romance'. *Journal of Popular Romance Studies*, 11, https://bit.ly/3Itn7OX. Accessed 27 June 2022.

Jackson, N. M. (2022). 'Freedom's Epilogue: Love as Freedom in Alyssa Cole's Historical Novellas'. *Journal of Popular Romance Studies*, 11, https://bit.ly/3lChshr. Accessed 27 June 2022.

Jagodzinski, M. (2014). 'We've Come a Long Way, Baby: Reflecting Thirty Years after *Reading the Romance*'. *Journal of Popular Romance Studies*, 4(2), https://bit.ly/3Ix1Vsj. Accessed 27 June 2022.

Jarmakani, A. (2020). 'Explorations of the "Desert Passions" Industry'. In J. Kamblé, E. Selinger & H. M. Teo, *The Routledge Research Companion to Popular Romance Fiction*, London: Routledge, pp. 252–66.

Jonaxx (2022). '@Jonaxx'. *Wattpad*, www.wattpad.com/user/jonaxx. Accessed 27 April 2022.

Jurilla, P. M. B. (2008). *Tagalog Bestsellers of the Twentieth Century: A History of the Book in the Philippines*, Manila: Ateneo de Manila University Press.

Kamblé, J. (2007). 'Female Enfranchisement and the Popular Romance: Employing an Indian Perspective'. In S. Goade, ed., *Empowerment versus*

Oppression: Twenty-First Century Views of Popular Romance Novels, Cambridge: Cambridge Scholars Press, pp. 148–73.

Kim, M. (2016). 'Gendered Migration and Filipino Women in Korea'. In N. Kim, ed., *Multicultural Challenges and Redefining Identity in East Asia*, London: Routledge, pp. 233–64.

Lacaba, J. F. (1983). 'Notes on "Bakya": Being an Apologia of Sorts for Filipino Masscult'. In R. M. Guerrero, ed., *Readings in Philippine Cinema*, Quezon City: Rapid Lithographic & Publishing House, pp. 117–23.

Lasco, G. (2020). *The Philippines Is Not a Small Country*, Manila: Ateneo de Manila University Press.

Leach, S. (2019). 'Romance is a Billion-Dollar Literary Industry. So Why Is It Still So Overlooked?' *Glamour*, 2 December, www.glamour.com/story/romance-is-a-billion-dollar-industry. Accessed 27 June 2022.

Lee, I. (2006). *Undercover Maid*, Quezon City: Bookware Publishing Corporation.

Lifestyle Inquirer (2015). 'Precious Pages Corp. Launches "25 Most Precious" Coffee-Table Book'. *Lifestyle.Inq*, 5 March, https://bit.ly/3EgXmQB. Accessed 4 April 2022.

Lim, R. S. & Bautista, B., eds. (2018). *Start Here: Short Stories of First Encounters*, Manila: RomanceClass.

Lit Hub (2020). 'The History of Romance Novels, a Billion Dollar Industry'. *Lit Hub*, 9 November, http://bit.ly/3YvOPBf. Accessed 27 June 2022.

Llanera, A. (2018). *Mango Summer*, Manila: Agay Llanera.

Lucero, R. C. (1991). 'Romancing the Otherness of Woman'. In S. S. Reyes, ed., *Reading Popular Culture*, Quezon City: Ateneo de Manila University Press, pp. 145–54.

Luczon, N. T. (2019). 'The Hugot That Is Kimi No Nawa: A Review of and Reflection on the Success of Your Name (2016) in the Philippines'. *Plaridel*, 16(2), 181–8.

Mangahas, M. (2022). 'Counting the Social Classes'. *Inquirer*, 10 September, https://opinion.inquirer.net/156855/counting-the-social-classes. Accessed 10 November 2022.

Mariano, C. (2014). *Cover Story Girl*, Manila: Chris Mariano.

Mariano, C. (2017). 'Drummer Boy'. In G. S. Gonzales, A. Llanera, C. Mariano, C. P. Sanit, J. E. Tria & I. Bautista-Yao, *Promdi Heart: Hometown Love Stories*, Manila: RomanceClass, n.p.

Markert, J. (1985). 'Romance Publishing and the Production of Culture'. *Poetics*, 14(1–2), 69–93.

Markert, J. (2016). *Publishing Romance: The History of an Industry, 1940s to the Present*, Jefferson, NC: McFarland.

Masallo, A. (2011). *How to Write a Tagalog Romance Novel*, Quezon City: Bookware Publishing Corporation.

McAlister, J., Parnell, C. & Trinidad, A. A. (2020). '#RomanceClass: Genre World, Intimate Public, Found Family'. *Publishing Research Quarterly*, 36(3), 403–17.

Meriz, H. (1985). *Bawal Kitmig Ibigin*, Quezon City: Books for Pleasure.

Mithen (2013). 'In Defense of Feels'. *The Fan Meta Reader*, 17 May, http://bit.ly/3EhD8Gl. Accessed 4 April 2022.

Moody-Freeman, J. E. (2020). 'African American Romance'. In J. Kamblé, E. Selinger & H. M. Teo, *The Routledge Research Companion to Popular Romance Fiction*, London: Routledge, pp. 229–51.

Moody-Freeman, J. E. (2022). 'Romance, Hip-Hop Feminism, and Black Love: From Theory to Praxis'. *Journal of Popular Romance Studies*, 11, https://bit.ly/3YFjewS. Accessed 27 June 2022.

Mori, B., de Borja, S. & de Guzman, C. (2019). *Alta: A High Society Romance Anthology*, Manila: RomanceClass.

Morrissey, K. (2014). 'Rattling the Toolkit: Methods for Reading Romance, Gender, and Culture'. *Journal of Popular Romance Studies*, 4(2), https://bit.ly/3IyB2EC. Accessed 27 June 2022.

Murray, S. (2012). *The Adaptation Industry: The Cultural Economy of Contemporary Literary Adaptation*, New York: Routledge.

National Book Development Board (2017). '2017 NBDB Readership Survey'. *National Book Development Board Philippines*, https://bit.ly/41fkx7I. Accessed 8 November 2022.

Noorda, R. & Marsden, S. (2019). 'Twenty-First Century Book Studies: The State of the Discipline'. *Book History*, 22(1), 370–97.

Ong, J. C. (2015). 'Introduction: The Poverty of Television'. In J. C. Corpus, ed., *The Poverty of Television: The Mediation of Suffering in Class-Divided Philippines*, London: Anthem Press, pp. 1–14.

Parnell, C. (2018). 'Models of Publishing and Opportunities for Change: Representations in Harlequin, Montlake and Self-Published Romance Novels'. *Australian Literary Studies*, 33(4), https://doi.org/10.20314/als.1cd73e2f68.

Parnell, C. (2021). 'Mapping the Entertainment Ecosystem of Wattpad: Platforms, Publishing and Adaptation'. *Convergence*, 27(2), 524–38.

Parnell, C. (2022). 'Platform Publishing and the Entertainment Ecosystem: Experiences of Marginalised Authors on Amazon and Wattpad', PhD Thesis, University of Melbourne.

Parnell, C., Trinidad, A. A. & McAlister, J. (2021a). 'Live Literature in the Philippines: An Ethnographic Study of #RomanceClass and Reading as Performance'. *Creative Industries Journal*, https://doi.org/10.1080/17510694.2021.1939544.

Parnell, C., Trinidad, A. A. & McAlister, J. (2021b). 'Hello, Ever After: #RomanceClass and Online-Only Live Literature in the Philippines in 2020'. *M/C Journal*, 24(3), https://bit.ly/3S5e1fB. Accessed 27 June 2022.

Pascual, M. (1985). *Laro ng Mga Puso*, Quezon City: Books for Pleasure.

Peralta, I. (2017). 'Where a "Promdi Heart" Goes (Part 1): An Interview with C. P. Santi and Ines Bautista-Yao'. *Bookbed: A Filipino Book Community*, 27 March, http://bit.ly/3KlbwnD. Accessed 14 April 2022.

Pertierra, A. C. (2021). 'Entertainment Publics in the Philippines'. *Media International Australia*, 179(1), 66–79.

Philippine Entertainment Portal (2014). 'She's Dating the Gangster Grosses P260 Million at the Box-Office'. *PEP.ph*, 9 August, http://bit.ly/3KezkcA. Accessed 24 June 2022.

Pop Fiction (2020). 'Jonaxx: Everything You Need To Know About MPress' Queen J'. *Pop Fiction Books*, 28 August, https://bit.ly/3YGbACu. Accessed 20 April 2022.

Precious Hearts. (2016). 'About Us'. *Precious Hearts Romance*, http://phr.com.ph/about-us/. Accessed 16 September 2021.

Pritchard, J. N. (2022). 'Reading the Black Romance: Exploring Black Sexual Politics in the Romance Fiction of Rebekah Weatherspoon'. *Journal of Popular Romance Studies*, 11, https://bit.ly/3KgFbhr. Accessed 27 June 2022.

Radyo Katipunan 87.9 (2021). *Sari-Sari | 21 Apr 21 Reading and Teaching Filipino Chick Lit and Contemporary Romance* [online video], https://youtu.be/_gZ5HhkklU4. Accessed 4 April 2022.

Raymundo, S. J. S. (2004). 'In the Concrete Now: Investigating Feminist Challenges to Popular Romance Production'. *Plaridel*, 1(2), 91–118.

Regis, P. (2003). *A Natural History of the Romance Novel*, Philadelphia: University of Pennsylvania Press.

Reyes, S. S. (1982). 'Ang Buhay-pamilya Sa Nobela, 1921–1944'. In S. Reyes, ed., *Nobelang Tagalog, 1905–1975: Tradisyon at modernismo*, Quezon City: Ateneo de Manila University, pp. 61–85.

Reyes, S. S. (1991). 'The Romance Mode in Philippine Popular Literature'. In S. Reyes, ed., *The Romance Mode in Philippine Popular Literature and Other Essays*, Manila: De La Salle University Press, pp. 23–39.

Reyes, S. S. (2001). 'Limang Pisong Pag-ibig: Isang Panimulang Pagsusuri'. In S. Reyes, ed., *Aliw: Selected Essays on Popular Culture*, Manila: De La Salle University Press, pp. 35–48.

Reyes, S. S. (2009). 'From Darna to ZsaZsa Zaturnnah: Desire and Fantasy'. In S. Reyes, ed., *From Darna to ZsaZsa Zaturnnah: Desire and Fantasy Essays on Literature and Popular Culture*, Pasig City: Anvil Publishing, pp. 2–34.

Reyes, S. S. (2012). 'Beyond Madonna and Magdalena: The Variety of Female Characters in Selected Popular Texts'. In S. Reyes, ed., *Narratives of Note: Studies of Popular Forms in the Twentieth Century*, Manila: University of Santo Tomas Publishing House, pp. 28–53.

Reyes, S. S. (2015). 'Part 2: The AlDub Experience: Millions Captivated'. *Rappler*, 31 October, http://bit.ly/3lCEKDT. Accessed 30 May 2022.

Reyles, Q. (2015). 'The Precious Story'. In Q. Reyles, ed., *25 Most Precious*, Quezon City: Precious Pages Corporation, pp. 8–13.

Ripped Bodice (2016). 'The State of Racial Diversity in Romance Publishing 2016'. *Ripped Bodice*, https://bit.ly/3XANtnr. Accessed 27 June 2022.

Ripped Bodice (2017). 'The State of Racial Diversity in Romance Publishing 2017'. *Ripped Bodice*, https://bit.ly/3jZMTSF. Accessed 27 June 2022.

Ripped Bodice (2018). 'The State of Racial Diversity in Romance Publishing 2018'. *Ripped Bodice*, https://bit.ly/3KeBPM0. Accessed 27 June 2022.

Ripped Bodice (2019). 'The State of Racial Diversity in Romance Publishing 2019'. *Ripped Bodice*, https://bit.ly/3Ech4Na. Accessed 27 June 2022.

Ripped Bodice (2020). 'The State of Racial Diversity in Romance Publishing 2020'. *Ripped Bodice*, https://bit.ly/3jZ8Wcd. Accessed 27 June 2022.

Rodriguez, C. Y. (2019). 'How We Do: #RomanceClass Covers'. *Chi Yu Rodriguez*, 3 August, http://chiyurodriguez.com/2019/08/03/how-we-do-romanceclasscovers/. Accessed 23 May 2022.

RomanceClass (n.d.a), 'About #romanceclass'. *#RomanceClass*, www .romanceclassbooks.com/about/. Accessed 1 April 2022.

RomanceClass (n.d.b). 'Start Here'. *#RomanceClass*, www.romanceclass books.com/book/start-here/. Accessed 29 March 2022.

RomanceClass (2020). *RomanceClass Q&A Session* [online video], https:// youtu.be/0oSAhTVleOk. Accessed 2 April 2022.

RomanceClass (2021). *RomanceClass Podcast S4 Episode 8 – The Philippines As Our Setting* [online video], https://youtu.be/l1xvfP3XPqg. Accessed 5 April 2022.

Rudisill, K. (2018). 'Full-Blooded Desi Romance: Contemporary English-Language Romance Novels in India'. *Journal of Popular Culture*, 51(3), 754–75.

RWA (n.d.). 'About the Romance Genre'. *Romance Writers of America*, www.rwa.org/Online/Romance_Genre/About_Romance_Genre.aspx. Accessed 18 April 2022.

Sagun, K. K. A. & Luyt, B. (2020). 'The Industry Avengers: An Analysis of Contemporary Comic Book Publishers in the Philippines'. *Convergence*, 26(1), 102–15.

Santi, C. P. (2016). *Dare to Love*, Manila: CP Santi.

Santi, C. P. (2017). 'Only the Beginning'. In *Promdi Heart: Hometown Love Stories*, Manila: RomanceClass, n.p.

Santiago, K. S. (2009). 'The Pinay As Fun, Fearless Female: Philippine Chick Literature in the Age of the Transnation'. *Humanities Diliman*, 6 (1–2), 57–92.

Santiago, K. S. (2018). *Romances: Variations on Love*, Manila: Ateneo de Naga University Press.

Santos, K. M. L. (2019). 'Disrupting Centers of Transcultural Materialities: The Transnationalization of Japan Cool through Philippine Fan Works'. *Mechademia: Second Arc*, 12(1), 96–117.

Schmid, W. (2013). 'Implied Reader'. *Living Handbook of Narratology*, 27 January, www.lhn.uni-hamburg.de/node/59.html. Accessed 27 June 2022.

Sering, T. F. T. (2002). *Getting Better*, Manila: Summit Books.

Sering, T. F. T. (2003). *Almost Married*, Manila: Summit Books.

Squires, C. (2017). 'Publishing's Diversity Deficit'. *CAMEo Cuts*, 2, 1–12.

Summit Books (2017). 'Summit Books' Majesty Press Imprint Releases Its First Book, *Heartless* by Jonaxx'. *Summit Media*, 10 August, www .summitmedia.com.ph/news/majesty-press-jonaxx-heartless. Accessed 20 April 2022.

Swartz, M. (2020). 'Vivian Stephens Helped Turn Romance into a Billion Dollar Industry. Then She Got Pushed Out'. *Texas Monthly*, September, http://bit.ly/3XH6dSl. Accessed 27 June 2022.

Tan, L. (2016). '"Kilig" Officially Added to Oxford English Dictionary'. *CNN Philippines*, 14 April, https://bit.ly/3Sn5uox. Accessed 4 April 2022.

Tapper, O. (2014). 'Romance and Innovation in Twenty-First Century Publishing'. *Publishing Research Quarterly*, 30(2), 249–59.

Taylor, J. (2007). 'And You Can Be My Sheikh: Gender, Race, and Orientalism in Contemporary Romance Novels'. *The Journal of Popular Culture*, 40(6), 1032–51.

Tejano, A. *et al.* (2017). *Make My Wish Come True*, Manila: RomanceClass.

Tejano, A., *et al.* (2022). *#RomanceClass NomCom: A Foodie Romance Anthology (Tropetastic Kindness Bundle #2)*, Manila: RomanceClass.

Teo, H. M. (2012). *Desert Passions: Orientalism and Romance Novels*, Austin: University of Texas Press.

Tindall, N. T. J. (2022). 'Black Romance Authors and Community Cultural Wealth: A Case Study of Brenda Jackson's Career'. *Journal of Popular Romance Studies*, 11, https://bit.ly/3ItRnt1. Accessed 27 June 2022.

Trinidad, A. A. (2018). '"Shipping" Larry Stylinson: What Makes Pairing Appealing Boys Romantic?' International Association for the Study of Popular Romance, Sydney, 27–29 June.

Trinidad, A. A. (2020). '"Kilig to the Bones!": Kilig as the Backbone of the Filipino Romance Experience'. International Association for the Study of Popular Romance, online conference.

Trinidad, C. (2018). *Ghost of a Feeling*, Manila: Celestine Trinidad.

Tupas, R. (2019). 'Entanglements of Colonialism, Social Class, and Unequal Englishes'. *Journal of Sociolinguistics*, 23, 529–42, https://doi .org/10.1111/josl.12384.

Tupas, R. & Lorente, B. P. (2014). 'A "New" Politics of Language in the Philippines: Bilingual Education and the New Challenge of the Mother Tongues'. In P. Sercombe & R. Tupas, eds., *Language, Education and Nation-Building: Assimilation and Shift in Southeast Asia*, London: Palgrave Macmillan, pp. 165–80.

Uparkar, S. (2014). 'Desi Love Stories: Harlequin Mills & Boon's Indian Enterprise'. *Australasian Journal of Popular Culture*, 3(3), 321–33.

Uy-Tioco, C. S. (2019). '"Good Enough" Access: Digital Inclusion, Social Stratification, and the Reinforcement of Class in the Philippines'. *Communication Research and Practice*, 5(2), 156–71. https://doi.org/ 10.1080/22041451.2019.1601492.

Valby, K. (2014). 'A Billion-Dollar Affair'. *Entertainment Weekly*, 17 October, https://ew.com/article/2014/10/17/billion-dollar-affair/. Accessed 27 June 2022.

Wattpad (2014). 'Hello, Pilipinas! Wattpad Partners With Summit Media'. *Wattpad*, 24 March, http://bit.ly/3EtGPZs. Accessed 22 February 2023.

Wattpad (2016). 'TV5 and Wattpad Presents: Original Stories Make It Big on the Small Screen'. *Wattpad*, 30 May, http://bit.ly/3xyXx5X. Accessed 20 May 2022.

We Are Social (2022). 'Digital 2022: Global Overview Report'. *We are Social and Hootesuite*, https://wearesocial.com/au/blog/2022/01/digital-2022/. Accessed 22 May 2022.

Wilkins, K., Driscoll, B. & Fletcher L. (2022). *Genre Worlds: Popular Fiction and Twenty-First Century Book Culture*, Amherst, MA: Massachusetts University Press.

Cambridge Elements ≡

Publishing and Book Culture

SERIES EDITOR
Samantha Rayner
University College London

Samantha Rayner is Professor of Publishing and Book Cultures at UCL. She is also Director of UCL's Centre for Publishing, co-Director of the Bloomsbury CHAPTER (Communication History, Authorship, Publishing, Textual Editing and Reading) and co-Chair of the Bookselling Research Network.

ASSOCIATE EDITOR
Leah Tether
University of Bristol

Leah Tether is Professor of Medieval Literature and Publishing at the University of Bristol. With an academic background in medieval French and English literature and a professional background in trade publishing, Leah has combined her expertise and developed an international research profile in book and publishing history from manuscript to digital.

ABOUT THE SERIES

This series aims to fill the demand for easily accessible, quality
texts available for teaching and research in the diverse and dynamic
fields of Publishing and Book Culture. Rigorously researched and
peer-reviewed Elements will be published under themes, or
'Gatherings'. These Elements should be the first check point for
researchers or students working on that area of publishing and book
trade history and practice: we hope that, situated so logically at
Cambridge University Press, where academic publishing in the UK
began, it will develop to create an unrivalled space where these
histories and practices can be investigated and preserved.

Cambridge Elements ☰

Publishing and Book Culture

Women, Publishing, And Book Culture

Gathering Editor: Nicola Wilson

Dr Nicola Wilson is Associate Professor in Book and Publishing Studies at the University of Reading and co-Director of the Centre for Book Cultures and Publishing. She specializes in twentieth-century print culture and literary history, publishers' archives, working-class writing, and histories of reading. She is currently working on a book about the British Book Society Ltd (1929–60) and is lead co-editor of *The Edinburgh Companion to Women in Publishing, 1900–2000* (EUP).

ELEMENTS IN THE GATHERING

Aboriginal Writers and Popular Fiction: The Literature of Anita Heiss
Fiannuala Morgan

Bluestockings and Travel Accounts: Reading, Writing and Collecting
Nataliia Voloshkova

Virago Reprints and Modern Classics: The Timely Business of Feminist Publishing
D-M Withers

Women and Letterpress Printing 1920–2020: Gendered Impressions
Claire Battershill

Publishing Romance Fiction in the Philippines
Jodi McAlister, Claire Parnell and Andrea Anne Trinidad

A full series listing is available at: www.cambridge.org/EPBC

Printed in the United States
by Baker & Taylor Publisher Services